Challenging the Gifted Child

Challenging the Gifted Child

An Open Approach to Working with Advanced Young Readers

MARGARET STEVENS

FOREWORD BY JUDITH HARE

Jessica Kingsley Publishers
London and Philadelphia

First published in 2009
by Jessica Kingsley Publishers
116 Pentonville Road
London N1 9JB, UK
and
400 Market Street, Suite 400
Philadelphia, PA 19106, USA

www.jkp.com

Library of Congress Cataloging in Publication Data
A CIP catalog record for this book is available from the Library of Congress

British Library Cataloguing in Publication Data
A CIP catalogue record for this book is available from the British Library

ISBN 978 1 84310 570 1

Printed and bound in Great Britain by
Printwise (Haverhill) Ltd, Suffolk

To Lucy,
whose love of nature
has been an inspiration.

My heartfelt thanks go to all who have helped me along the road and in particular to the following: Dr Farouk Walji and the late Mrs Frieda Painter for encouraging me to write; Dr Edward Chitham for his vote of confidence in my Open Way; the Buckinghamshire Library and Information Service to Schools for vital initial inspiration, and the staff of the Public Library for their untiring assistance; Corbett's Bookshops, Princes Risborough, for patiently tracking down unusual titles; the many educators, parents and children who have shared with me their enthusiasm for my courses; The Potential Trust and Tomorrow's Achievers for grants kindly supplied to families; the National Association for Gifted Children for suggesting this book, and especially Mrs Jane Hughes for her keen interest and constant encouragement; and of course my late husband, Geoffrey, for his love and support always.

Contents

List of Resources

Resources (at the ends of chapters)

Further Resources (at the end of the book)

Foreword

It was in February 2001 that I first met with Margaret.

I had been appointed Adviser for Gifted and Talented Pupils in the London Borough of Lambeth (working within the UK Government's 'Excellence in Cities' scheme), and was looking for a program that would challenge the language abilities of the pupils for whom I was responsible. Above all, I was looking for something user-friendly to offer teachers.

I had come across an article first published in Margaret's Open Way Newsletter and afterwards in the magazine of the National Association for Gifted Children (NAGC). In it a parent, herself a professional, described how Open Way courses had helped her seven-year-old avid reader to find more books and to think about what he was reading.

As soon as I set eyes on the courses I knew I wanted to capture them for the classroom. I asked Margaret to adapt, in time for the new academic year, materials for use by seven- to eight-year-olds.

Meanwhile we ran one of her existing courses with a couple of pupils then reaching the end of that year-stage, and I remember asking these how the work was going and being met with puzzled frowns. They had not thought of the program as 'work'. It was 'fun' they said!

Margaret's courses were rapidly extended to cover ages five through eleven, and during the years that I was in a position to offer a course to any of my schools, for children needing this kind of challenge at any point, I was able to quote further positive response in my own newsletter:

'The books are so good I don't skip pages any more.'

'I used to hate reading even though I was good at it, and only read when I had to. Now I can't go to bed without reading a chapter of my book first.'

'All the books are so good they are so much better than the books in the library.'

'I really like it because you get to read loads of different books but they are all about the same kind of thing and they all fit together.'

'I like the opportunity to read books that are much more exciting than what I normally read. I know they are stretching me and they make me think much more too.'

As author, Margaret was under contract to Lambeth Council, and a contract was written that claimed 'the raising of self-esteem' as one of the chief objectives, alongside more obvious targets, such as higher levels in official national tests. During this time I agreed to a non-exclusive licence so that schools in other parts of the country could benefit from what was on offer.

Sadly the contract came to an end after five years when there were changes in government funding. Schools have continued to benefit from whatever materials and books they had already, and Margaret has carried on with Open Way courses for families and individual schools elsewhere in the country.

This book, *Challenging the Gifted Child*, is accessible to all who have the task of educating highly intelligent children, or those underachieving, in the realm of literature and language. I have no hesitation in recommending it as a guide to both theory and practice.

Judith Hare,
School Improvement Adviser & Team Leader,
Inclusion & Standards, Lambeth

Preface

More than one person has said, 'It's a pity you didn't do all this twenty-five years ago.' Truth is… it has taken a lifetime to provide me with the necessary know-how and the confidence to share it with others.

As a child I read early and books became my delight. I was allowed comics, the *Beano* and the *Dandy*. Books were scarce, dear, and much treasured. I survived chiefly on classics from the library. At home, I sat reading on a broad sill behind the curtains; at boarding-school, under the bedclothes!

Reading aloud was a strong family tradition. My mother read us the much-loved tales of Beatrix Potter. My father later made us laugh with *Three Men in a Boat*. In summer our grandmother read to us in her garden.

I was 16 when my parents, Paul and Charlotte, opened their small school for children who had poor health and consequent personal problems. Charlotte was doctor and housekeeper; Paul was in charge of the teaching. I lived alongside the venture in holidays and spent a 'gap-year' there before university.

Although I rarely helped Paul in the schoolroom I must have derived inspiration from his out-of-the-ordinary teaching methods and materials, provided by the Parents' National Education Union. People have fond memories of that schoolroom. My father was admired and respected, the atmosphere happy and relaxed.

My own education continued at Keele University where my principal subjects were English and German, with subsidiary Russian and Physics. Everyone did a foundation year on the history of Western civilization. This broadened our outlook and helped us appreciate the interests of students in other fields.

As a teacher I joined the junior Remedial Department of a growing 'city-fringe' Bilateral School and taught 'reluctant readers'! After three years' valuable in-service training I went on to teach country children and later still encountered island children. I also spent two years in industry as a technical translator, and did other jobs at various times, including home tuition for our district education authority, and privately.

My initial five years in so-called 'remedial' teaching got me into a year's course in what is now Special Needs. And there I heard of the National Association for Gifted Children (NAGC).

In 1981 my own child was born. As we gradually came to recognize our son's high ability, I knew where to turn and contacted NAGC. I had 17 years as full-time mum behind me when I began writing, including the two years when my son was learning outside of secondary school.

In 1998 I was asked to write a correspondence course in English for gifted children. I revised on child development, devoured huge numbers of children's books, and discovered how to use a computer!

What I came up with, however, was not the formal English course that had been expected! That is how I came to run my own Open Way Language and Literature Courses for Advanced Young Readers – courses that I and others have been using with great success ever since. And now it is time to pass on my expertise.

Introduction

The happiness of the child is the condition of his progress.

Charlotte Mason 1842–1923

You have picked up this book so you have an interest in challenging the gifted child. Perhaps you are a would-be educator, or an educator already engaged in trying to meet the needs of a known child or group. Are any of these you?

- You were not a keen reader, but your daughter has her nose permanently buried in a book.

- You preferred encyclopedias to stories and you want a better balance for your son.

- You want to wean your children off 'screen time' and give them a love of literature.

- You are a principal or head teacher with a strong perception of exceptionally able children as 'special needs'.

- You are a class teacher with one or more pupils reading well ahead of target.

- You are training teachers and are open to any new approach.

If so, then this book is for you. The focus is on the 'advanced young reader'. The aim is to enable readers to devise and implement courses for themselves. In *Challenging the Gifted Child* I share what I have discovered about the way fast readers and quick thinkers often prefer to learn, and describe my tried-and-tested materials, which are innovative because they stress learning rather than teaching and actually provide for, rather than simply acknowledge, the needs of the child and the child's right of choice.

After each chapter and also at the end of the book I have given resources to aid you in 'course-building'. These are simply relevant samples taken from my tried-and-tested materials.

Choose to work with what best fits your situation:

- the underlying principles
- the objectives of pupil enthusiasm and growth in confidence
- my advice on books, open challenges and running a home or school course
- the resources as adaptable models.

Background

In 1998 I was approached about writing a distance-learning English course specifically designed for the gifted child. Not realizing that something very formal was envisaged, I responded with a choice of books for 'advanced young readers', with follow-up that allowed for a free response from the child and sympathetic mentoring from an adult.

This new more fluid approach was warmly received by the National Association for Gifted Children (NAGC), so I decided to use the materials myself and, in April 1999, started my own organization, The Open Way.

I chose 'The Open Way' to suggest a choice of path, and had a logo of a child opening a door and letting in sunlight. Open Way's first customers were individual children at home aged 4 to 8, but its principles can be applied at any age. School-based courses followed in 2002 and were extended to meet the needs of all through to the age of 11. This book is created with the 4- to 11-year-old age range in mind.

The children
What is a 'gifted' child?

I equate 'gifted' with the term 'exceptionally able' used by educational psychologists to imply a higher degree of learning ability than either 'able' (noticeably above the norm) or 'very able' (more so). But 'able children' can be used as an umbrella term for all three levels, making it more difficult to draw attention to the special needs of the exceptionally able child, and those of the very highest intelligence, sometimes referred to as 'profoundly able' for whom the system scarcely provides. The fact is that a gifted child's intelligence can be a matter not simply of *degree* but also of *kind*, with learning skills that indicate advanced and varied thought processes; and the greater the intelligence the more marked the differences become, until one is dealing with individuals of extremely rare ability.

Recognizing gifted children is never straightforward, and providing for them is unfortunately not just a matter of rushing ahead into work planned for later age-levels. Even when governments provide official definitions of giftedness, their statements tend to fall short of the needs of those with the very highest intelligence; also schools are still expected to see to identification and provision for the percentage that government has set its sights on. The box below shows how giftedness is officially defined for educational purposes, in the USA, the UK and Canada.

Official Definitions of Giftedness in the USA, UK and Canada

USA (quoted with permission)

The current federal definition of gifted students, included in the *Elementary and Secondary Act*, is:

> Students, children, or youth who give evidence of high achievement capability in areas such as intellectual, creative, artistic or leadership capacity, or in specific academic fields, and who need services and activities not ordinarily provided by the school in order to fully develop those capabilities.

Note: States and districts are not required to use the federal definition, although many states base their definitions on the federal definition.

UK

The present UK government (March 2007) admits that there are many definitions of 'gifted and talented', but the Department for Education and Skills, identifying around 10 per cent of children within the current education system as 'Gifted and Talented', presents its own definition to parents, in the context of the 'Gifted and Talented Strand' of Excellence in Cities:

> The Department for Education and Skills defines 'gifted' pupils as those who have exceptional abilities in one or more subjects in the statutory school curriculum other than art and design, music and PE. 'Talented' pupils are defined as those who have exceptional abilities in art and design, music, PE or in sports or performing arts such as dance and drama.

Canada

In Canada, provinces have jurisdiction over education, so definitions will vary. The Ministry of Education British Columbia uses the following definition:

> A student is considered gifted when she/he possesses demonstrated or potential abilities that give evidence of exceptionally high capability with respect to intellect, creativity, or the skills associated with specific disciplines. Students who are gifted often demonstrate outstanding abilities in more than one area. They may demonstrate extraordinary intensity of focus in their particular areas of talent or interest. However, they may also have accompanying disabilities and should not be expected to have strengths in all areas of intellectual functioning.

Where performance within the school system is the gauge given by the government, schools should at least be able to recognize high achievers. Hopefully they will also be on the lookout for 'underachievers', and be aware that giftedness embraces children who gain more attention as 'dyslexic' but are frequently gifted in curriculum subjects such as mathematics and engineering, or talented in drama, art or design. It is crucial to recognize and applaud these children's high intelligence, otherwise their image of themselves will be as 'reading failures'. (A relatively recent push to reconsider dyslexia as the 'flip-side' of a strongly visual process of perception, a 'gift' in itself, should be of help in this regard.)

This book, however, is for those whose *strength* is reading. Why? Well, adults often fail to understand that children who are reading well also need encouragement. Success comes from building on and encouraging a child's strengths, not taking them for granted.

Advanced young readers

Who qualifies as an 'advanced young reader'? Below are some examples of those who have fallen into this category:

- the 6-year-old who could work with a higher grade if not so emotionally immature
- the 9-year-old who reads well and also writes promising poetry
- the tiresome underachiever aged 7 or 8 who is either much cleverer than he knows or is cleverer than he is prepared to admit
- your 6-year-old child who is reading three years ahead at home while you wait to find a new school when you move
- your daughter of 8 who is happy at an independent school but only reads non-fiction
- the highly intelligent boy aged 11 whose mother promised you a medal if you could get him to read anything but Roald Dahl!
- your highly perceptive child whose physical condition makes home-schooling a better option
- the child who, on starting school, is rapidly taking to reading in English although English is not the first language of her parents.

Some others who could qualify:

- the silent reader who is mistaken for a non-reader because everyone else is reading aloud at this level and it is assumed that he is just looking at the pictures
- the child who is turned off reading by the prescriptive list that has to be got through book by book, completing each stage before moving up to the next (can look like a reluctant reader)
- the dreamer who makes up stories from the illustrations because he has already read the book cover to cover three times and is waiting for a chance to ask for another!

- the girl who realizes she is reading too fast and so learns to read upside down in order to read aloud to her friends while they look at the pictures right way up!

- the boy aged 10 who hangs around after class to ask the penetrating questions he is reluctant to ask during lessons

- the girl who is three or four years into school and conforming to all that is asked of her there but at home reveals she is way ahead of that standard

- the 'reluctant writer'!

- and the child on whose account you are reading this book...?

The advantage of using the term 'advanced' is that a teacher can build a group to include any who are reading sufficiently far ahead of the norm to benefit from the input and approach at the same time as catering for gifted individuals whose ability is far above the norm.

I started by writing for children reading three years ahead, and have catered for individuals whose reading age was higher, but soon realized a less advanced level was also useful. This version proved right for some pupils at home, and also enabled me to make the schools' versions flexible, when it became clear that schools needed to organize small groups of 'very good readers' in which an 'exceptional reader' could feel comfortable. I discuss the size and make-up of school groups in Chapter 5.

Parents came to me asking how to find enough books and the right kind of books. Teachers, too, were grateful for this kind of help. Both welcomed a program that encouraged not just reading but also more thinking.

The philosophy
The focus on reading and away from other problems

A focus on reading ability helps teachers, because it is easy and acceptable to use the category of 'advanced young reader' to decide, without the official assessment of an educational psychologist, who will benefit from the materials and the approach.

Avid readers are naturally delighted with extra books. School pupils are relieved to be enrolled in a group rather than singled out. Those at home are happier with more to read after school, at weekends or in the holidays. Books are often central in home education anyway, and the open approach is welcome and manageable.

A child identified as having a physical disability or health problem, or a condition that affects their behaviour (such as ADHD, Asperger's Syndrome, dyspraxia, or Tourette's Syndrome), can sadly be looked upon as 'special educational needs' without reference to his or her intelligence. Parents familiar with this situation are naturally relieved to have their child congratulated on an area of strength and achievement. Professor Diane Montgomery has drawn attention to this kind of 'double exceptionality' in her book *Gifted and*

Talented Children with Special Educational Needs: Double Exceptionality – Identify Highly Able Pupils with SEN (ADHD, Dyspraxia, Dyslexia & Downs Syndrome) (David Fulton Publishers, 2003).

Structuring the learning environment

With a growing emphasis on the value of what are now commonly referred to as 'higher-order thinking skills', there is a welcome realization that 'challenging' is meant to be something other than the old (somewhat mind-boggling) idea that 'the brighter child needs stretching'. Benjamin Bloom, in his renowned *Taxonomy of Educational Objectives* (1956), defines these higher-order skills as 'the cognitive, affective and psychomotor aspects of the learning process' – those skills that take the learner beyond the mere acquisition of facts.

On the basis that a child reckoned to be highly intelligent and already reading well deserves further challenge and success:

- Why not present pupils with beautiful and interesting books that challenge them without being emotionally 'beyond their years'?

- Why not release them from the burden of an expected response?

- The appointed mentor ought surely to listen, without criticism or undue comment?

- Is it helpful to force an answer or coerce into creative writing?

- Isn't what is needed an 'openness' that goes beyond what teachers know as 'differentiation'?

This approach has been incorporated in the Open Way principles:

1. That, with *free access* to the books as the starting-point, a broad foundation of reading experience is best provided by seeking out a wide variety of titles – stories, non-fiction, poetry and plays – that are carefully juxtaposed, and may share a common theme such as 'Sun, Wind and Rain' for younger readers or 'Exploration' for an older child.

2. That a *free response* should be allowed for. If circumstances allow, a verbal response can be written down by the supervising adult; or an interview can be staged and recorded. No child should be prompted to write, only invited.

3. That criticism and correction based on planned outcomes should be abandoned in favour of this free response, which (however minimal at first) should in turn be met with *maximum acceptance*. Praise and encouragement are needed at all times, more especially where there is a need to restore self-esteem.

4. That 'questions' are abandoned in favour of '*challenges*' where the answers depend on the child's observation and judgement. Spaces provided for

responses, including Open Challenge Pages provided for schools, are designed in this way and demand higher-order thinking skills.

5. That *creative writing* be 'allowed for' rather than demanded, although experience has shown that writing will follow reading as confidence grows.

What is to be your role?

This book is about what an open approach entails for both child *and adult.*

Creating a course will make you an author, and so I give guidelines on how to create a structure that will:

- present a wide choice of challenging yet age-appropriate books
- assist learning and creativity
- be right for now, and then 'build' over the years.

If your program is to be run by someone else, then it is a good idea to put in a framework that will assist the child's response and make it easy for the adult to give positive comment and record progress. I will explain how these needs might be met.

If you are yourself aiding the day-to-day progress of one or more children, then your role will be that of 'mentor'. You might simply bring together sets of books chosen by topic, but a framework will put things more firmly into the hands of the learner and help keep you from adopting a 'teaching role'.

Chapter 1 outlines the basic features of an Open Way program. The chapters that follow explain the significance of the approach and illustrate further how to enrich your child's learning.

What is a mentor?

A mentor is someone who 'accompanies the child on a journey', in this case a journey through literature and language. In contrast to 'teacher' or 'tutor' it is a term that seems to put pupils more in charge of their learning. It is for this reason that I will use the term 'mentor' throughout my book.

Gifted children need *your* answers to *their* questions. This is their challenge to you as mentor:

- The mentor is there to respond to the child's opinions and questions.
- The mentor should be someone to share with, to bounce ideas off; someone to rely on for helpful comment on the pupil's reaction to the books.

Some kind of response should be forthcoming from the mentor. It can be written if the child's response is written but must be in line with the principle of praise and encouragement.

Schools certainly need an adult mentor but live discussion is usually the way forward. In Chapter 5 I explain more about how to give the child the lead.

Reading – the way forward

Reading, whether as an end in itself or as a means to an end, is meant above all to be enjoyable!

A child that reads well needs more than to be constantly on the receiving end of instruction, especially in a class that covers a wide range of ability. True progress will come from careful guidance and a special program, providing not only a broad foundation for a lifetime's enjoyment of books, but also a way into independent learning and research.

In an earlier age, reading was the generally accepted way of learning, and many a well-known book has a character in it who is an avid reader. Take Louisa May Alcott's Jo in *Little Women* or Susan Coolidge's Katy.

Jane Austen also writes in *Mansfield Park* (1814) of how rich young ladies were taught at home by a governess (Miss Lee). Not so the 'poor relation' Fanny who was lucky that her cousin Edmund recognized her ability, provided her with good books and praised her efforts:

> His attentions were…of the highest importance in assisting the improvement of her mind and extending its pleasures. He knew her to be clever, to have a quick apprehension as well as good sense, and a fondness for reading, which, properly directed must be an education in itself. Miss Lee taught her French, and heard her read the daily portion of history; but he recommended the books which charmed her leisure hours, he encouraged her taste, and corrected her judgement: he made reading useful by talking to her of what she read, and heightened its attraction by judicious praise.

This goes to show that reading is a sound basis for learning and that the Open Way principles of praise, encouragement and choice have roots going back a couple of centuries at least.

Chapter 1

Building Your Course

The flame of freedom in their souls,
And light of knowledge in their eyes.

John Addington Symonds 1840–1893

In this chapter I give you a glimpse of the likely end-product, by outlining the essentials of the course you will be empowered to implement. I set out the basic framework or structure; the function of topics and modules; the importance of the books chosen; and the avenues of response you will create for your child or students.

Basic Structure

Units, books and topics

Every Open Way course is made up of units presented to the child one at a time.

- A *unit* should be taken as a whole, and may last from two to four weeks, depending on the time designated, and also on the amount of time it takes to gather together and read the necessary books.

- Every unit depends on its list of *whole books*. (Books are discussed in detail in Chapter 4.)

- The book choice for each unit is suggested by a *topic*, which can be for that unit only (as recommended for younger children) or in turn belong to a module (for older students), possibly one that concentrates either on fiction or on non-fiction instead of mixing the two. A *module* can last for a longer period and comprise between eight and twelve units held together by a theme such as 'Explorers' (age 9+).

- Topics are intended first and foremost to appeal and awaken interest, and to provide an 'umbrella' for the books. (Chapter 3 offers you ideas for topics and modules, and possible overall themes, not only for the older student but also to hold together the one-unit-one-topic schedule that suits younger children. I say more about the nature and value of an 'overall theme' below.)

Samples illustrating the basic make-up of a typical unit are given in Resource 1.1 'Topics and Books' at the end of this chapter.

Teaching Text

Another feature you may want to include in your course is called a Teaching Text. It is a way of drawing children in to the topic and books by telling them a little bit about them, in a conversational and informal tone. This can be especially valuable in that it

- allows children to take the lead in their own learning
- allows you, the course-writer, to delegate the running of the program to a colleague.

In Chapter 3 I explain a bit more about Teaching Texts. There is also a sample in the resources at the end of this chapter.

An overall theme

YOUNGER CHILDREN

Units, with their topics and books, can be embraced by a theme covering a period of time, such as a grade or year-stage; at home a chosen theme may be shortened or extended to coincide with the child's interests, progress and development.

In Chapters 3 and 6 I mention how children love the feeling of adventure involved in 'making a journey', and how making such a journey together helps the sharing of child with adult. The journey idea also allows each unit of your program to be seen as a stage in a whole, moving forward in terms of one unit leading on to another.

OLDER CHILDREN

The overall theme for a year could be let's say 'The Environment' or 'Planet Earth' (9+) or 'People' (10+). Such a theme can easily cover three or more modules, such as a story module, a non-fiction module, and one that embraces poetry and plays. Chapter 2 will tell you why this could be important in terms of 'reading experience'.

Obtaining a response

In the Introduction I stressed the importance of encouragement, and acceptance of a child's views. You will find the reasons for this fully explained in Chapters 2 and 3, but every chapter in this book has something to say about how children can be encouraged to respond happily and without coercion, letting you in on their feelings and opinions. I discuss, particularly in Chapter 3, how to avoid having a planned outcome, which amounts to a form of prescription by the adult.

You need only create a channel for a child's response and there are two main ways of achieving this. The first, coming either spread out within the Teaching Text or following straight after, will appear to consist of questions, but closer examination will reveal that each has no right or wrong answer. These are what I call Open Challenges (see Resource 1.2 at the end of this chapter). I explain more about these in the second half of Chapter 3, where I also give typical examples across the age-range. You will find more as you explore the resources.

At the end section of your unit you have a second channel for response – the Free Space pages, these being for the already keen writer and for the 'writer still to become inspired'. Resource 1.3 at the end of this chapter illustrates how to provide for this completely free type of response. Having two whole pages means that one can be geared to the content of the unit and one totally open. Both can be presented in a way that will appeal to the age range of the child.

By the end of Chapter 4 you will have sufficient information to be able to begin structuring your units and your course as a whole. Chapter 5 is about the practicalities of organizing and running a course in various situations. Chapter 6 takes a look at how your units and course as a whole will allow you to give subtle and appropriate language teaching, and examines what the task of writing actually involves. Chapter 7 has some concluding thoughts on the book as a whole, and gives some examples of inspired writing that have come from children on Open Way courses.

Resource 1.1 Topics and Books, Unit 1: Just Imagine! (Age 6)

Name _____ Date _____

Key Books (for this unit and the rest at this level)

Dictionary (DK)

Encyclopedia (DK)

My First Oxford Book of Poems

The King's Pyjamas ed. Pie Corbett

Now We Are Six by A.A. Milne

Four o'Clock Friday by John Foster

. . . .

Part 1. Wild animals, ordinary people

NON-FICTION – Choose from these:

Easy:

Imagine You Are a Dolphin (or a *Tiger* or an *Orang-Utan*) by Karen Wallace

Harder:

Whale Journey; Swallow Journey; Caribou Journey by Vivian French

STORIES

Bernard Ashley: *A Present for Paul*

Jenny Nimmo: *Ronnie and the Giant Millipede*

Longer STORIES

Jamila Gavin: *Fine Feathered Friend* (Yellow Bananas)

Michael Morpurgo: *Colly's Barn* (Yellow Bananas)

POETRY

The King's Pyjamas p. 42 and p. 43

. . . .

Part 2. And finally extraordinary everything

STORIES again

Michael Foreman: *Grandfather's Pencil and the Room of Stories*

Jeff Brown: *Flat Stanley*

Dick King-Smith: *George Speaks*

Roald Dahl: *The Giraffe and the Pelly and Me*

Or something you choose

POETRY

in *My First Oxford Book of Poems* p. 76 and p. 77

in *The King's Pyjamas* p. 40

Resource 1.2 Teaching Text, Unit 1: Just Imagine! (Age 6)

Extract from: Part 1. Wild animals, ordinary people

You are using your imagination all the time, you know. You use it to think about what is going to happen tomorrow or next week or when your uncle comes to see you. You may use it to imagine what you will get for your birthday.

Sometimes someone comes and tells you something that has already taken place but you were not there. Your friend's dog was sick on the carpet! That's not something imaginary. It's true. (Maybe your friend's mother wishes it wasn't!) But you still have to imagine it because you were not there.

Some things are going on all the while in other places all over the world, even under the sea. In a moment you will get a chance to find out how imaginative you are. But first use your special dictionary to look up 'imagination' and other words connected with it, like 'imagine' and 'imaginary'.

Now look for a book in the first (NON-FICTION) part of your list: Imagine you are that animal. Can you get inside its skin?

Now for something about your FICTION stories.

The author who writes a made-up story has to imagine it, of course!

When you read the story you imagine you are inside the pages of the book sharing in what happens there.

It may be a fairly ordinary story about families or schools or exploring in your vacation. You still have to imagine it all happening…

Extract from: Part 2. And finally extraordinary everything

…What else can all of us do with our imaginations?

Here are three common expressions:

'a leap of the imagination'

'a huge stretch of the imagination'

'someone's imagination running riot'
[Two more later]

Your second group of STORIES will begin by raising your eyebrows and end by making you gasp. Your mouth will drop open and your eyes will pop out of your head at the impossible things the authors have decided will happen.

You have to agree to join in, and believe everything could really be like that (just between the first and last pages of the book, you understand)!

…Take the first storybook on your Book List.

It's written by Michael Foreman, who is both author and illustrator. So it's a picture book. Remember that the pictures may be carrying some of the story.

Notice which people and things appear in the story. Decide if any of it could be true.

Does it exercise your imagination?

There are three more stories on your list each one more incredible than the last. They will have your imagination working overtime!

Resource 1.3 Free Space Pages (All Ages)

Unit _ _ _ _ _ _ _ _ _ _ _ _ _ _   Week _ _ _ _ _ _ _ _ _ _ _ _ _ _ _ _

SAY IN YOUR OWN WAY

Name _ _ _ _ _ _ _ _ _ _ _ _   Class _ _ _ _ _ _ _ _ _ _ _ _ _ _ _ _

Something about dolphins or whales? Or about other wild creatures?

Something about funny books?

Something about books with strange happenings in them?

Or something else?

_ _

_ _

_ _

_ _

_ _

_ _

Unit _ _ _ _ _ _ _ _ _ _ _ _ _ _ _ _ _   Week_ _ _ _ _ _ _ _ _ _ _ _ _ _ _ _ _ _ _

WRITE or TELL

Name _ _ _ _ _ _ _ _ _ _ _ _ _ _ _ _   Class_ _ _ _ _ _ _ _ _ _ _ _ _ _ _ _ _ _

_ _

_ _

_ _

_ _

_ _

_ _

_ _

_ _

_ _

_ _

Chapter 2

Reading and Responding

Dreams, books are each a world.

William Wordsworth 1770–1850

Reading will be the starting-point of your course and the children's chief inspiration. In this chapter, therefore, I look at all the different ways of reading and the types of readers there are. I then detail some of the many and varied ways that children may respond to what they have read, and how adults can encourage their responses.

Reading

The reading experience

Before you start searching for books for your course, it is worth finding out how good readers, and yours in particular, experience reading. Where children are invited to reveal in simple ways the various reading situations they enjoy, it makes them feel in charge of the new venture, with a mentor who is truly interested in them and what they read. At the same time, the mentor can use the child's answers as a diagnostic, noting at what level and in what areas the child is currently enjoying reading.

At the end of this chapter there are resource samples showing different ways of doing this. Resources 2.1 and 2.2 show how it is possible to get feedback from children even as young as 4 or 5:

- either in school, by using a checklist in your unit itself
- or from a child of similar age at home, using a questionnaire.

Each of these allows for plenty of thought with little or no demand in terms of writing. The second method, the questionnaire, can be adapted for use with any age of child, and is extremely useful in assessing where that child stands in relation to reading, possibly also writing, and drawing them to a course.

The oral questionnaire for ages 7 to 8 given at the end of this chapter (Resource 2.3) was designed to allow teachers an insight into how far individual schoolchildren are interested in and involved with books. It was first used to record results to judge later whether pupils had become more thinking readers and better acquainted with books by the end of the initial course-stage.

Such methods can also help the adult uncover any attitude towards reading or writing that it will be helpful to take note of and work around. A child who feels the adult-in-charge is sincere and involved will be willing and unafraid to share whatever is on their mind. One home-schooling 6-year-old, when asked, 'What writing do you do?', answered in neat handwriting and with perfect spelling, 'As little as possible'!

Have you noticed that when you try to refocus a child's interest you often sense resistance? You may see that child as inattentive, whereas he or she is more likely just preoccupied. In Open Way terms such as preoccupation or distraction can be reinterpreted as an opportunity and used as a chance for the child to learn about taking a responsible lead. If an excited child wants to tell you how their tooth came out and the tooth fairy left a coin under their pillow, it is wise not to be dismissive. Sharing their enthusiasm you might encourage them to talk a little more about tooth fairies. On no account force this, and if writing is an option let them choose whether they or you do the writing.

Reading and maturity

Everyone knows that stories at home, on rainy days and at bedtime, have been loved for generations. Sharing books is still valuable for those who can read alone.

It is very easy to expect a 'clever' or 'bright' child to be advanced in every way. Lost in amazement at the child's reading ability and intellectual progress, we may not realize that, emotionally and socially, a gifted child may in fact be lagging behind chronological peers. This could be for many reasons. Perhaps they have gone ahead at speed on the cognitive front and have given less attention to perceiving the behavioural patterns of their age-group peers. Perhaps they feel in need of reassurance, having found themselves continually misunderstood or underappreciated. If your young advanced reader wants to listen to you read, or sit and share a book, let them be their age, rather than insist that they should read to you, or read to themselves.

Most children look forward to a story at the end of a school day. If a gifted child's attention wanders from a simple tale chosen to suit the class as a whole, then a slightly more challenging story on audiotape or CD with headphones may provide an answer. To keep the element of sharing, however, and avoid a problem with peers, a group should be created to listen together and discuss. A gifted child can so easily feel a misfit, and the

CHALLENGING THE GIFTED CHILD

damage in terms of low self-esteem is more serious and long-lasting than many are prepared to recognize.

That said, wanting to listen may also mean that the child will be a good listener through life. Some people remember best what they hear. They are 'auditory learners'.

Others may be 'visual learners' needing to pore over books to absorb their contents. These visual learners will still want you around to take an interest, answer questions and lead them on to other books. (A good non-fiction book should give rise to further questions.)

Huge amounts of valuable information can be found on the internet but, as everyone knows, this needs careful handling and ties children to the computer. Also, one site can lead to another until the task becomes daunting and seemingly never-ending. The particular value of a book is that it is both portable and contained. There is a certain satisfaction in handling it, and the child can close it with a sense of achievement after the last page is read. Books can also help a child to sleep. A 9-year-old once told me he always read poetry at bedtime because it made him peaceful.

In Chapter 4, I discuss in some detail the various kinds of books there are and explain how to choose a range to match a given topic, thus providing a reading experience with both breadth and depth. I discuss content and style, and how to achieve a balance between some titles that are imaginative and others that are informative. Publishers, authors and illustrators are discussed as well.

The child as reader

Silent reading is considered the ultimate skill, but in the past everyone read aloud. So if children want to read aloud – let them! Don't we all like to share a good poem or an interesting fact?

A child saying, 'Listen to this!' may be saying, 'Look how well I read!' or may wish to share what the book is about. A mother might have to counsel patience if she is on the phone or changing the baby. A teacher might be on her way to see the principal, or aware the child is missing lunch. But do acknowledge the need and meet it as soon as possible.

I was once asked to wait in the library of a well-known school for gifted children. A girl of 7 or 8 was sitting on a stool engrossed in her book. The minute she saw me she offered to read me a story. 'Yes, *please!*' I said, and she embarked on 'How the Whale Became' by Ted Hughes, reading with expression and drawing me in. After a while she stopped to see how many more pages there were and remarked, 'This is rather long, but I've read it before so I could just tell you about it if you like?' I was sorry I had to go before we had done.

Good readers in a class may have to wait while the teacher listens to those who have not yet got there. In that case they deserve something really challenging and worthwhile to read otherwise they will very likely play down their ability, and either withdraw or become disruptive. A mother with a 5-year-old carrying the 'Asperger's' label had tried in vain to make his nursery school aware how well he was reading at home. When the school called her in after a class trip to the park she wondered what her son had been up to. Had he pushed someone into the pond? No! He had read all the obscene graffiti scrawled on the park benches! At least the teachers were now happy to acknowledge his reading ability.

Reading independently

In the earliest school years not all fluent readers are alike in their experience of books. While all can now recognize or decode words at speed, some may have started reading at 2 or 3 years old, while others rocketed away on entering school.

Also, those from a home where books are cherished and available will initially have an advantage over others whose home background or culture is less 'book-centred'.

Where there are few books in the home it is important that creators of a school course, for instance, give guidance on choosing extra books at school or in the public library. The same goes for children where the parent does not have English as a first language or is not familiar with children's literature in English.

Parent involvement was always part of my own courses for schools. Why?

- By asking families to help search for books you are saying how important reading is for the child.

- Parents who value books will still welcome guidance and may even help to provide books for a school-based course.

Understanding – word level

It is rare for an established reader not to be able to decipher a word even if the meaning is unclear. All readers are prepared to skate over one or two unfamiliar words rather than interrupt the flow. An unknown word can be understood provided it sits within a context of five already familiar words.

Words taken direct from another language, such as *hors d'oeuvre* or *vermicelli* can prove a stumbling block. The mentor should discuss the meaning of words as they arise, but not anticipate or take over.

Book choices

The joy of being able to read well is that technically speaking you can read 'anything'.

But to be interesting and enjoyable a book must *reach* you. One written for children with more years of growth and life-experience may not be 'age-appropriate' and this really matters.

Experience has shown that the hardest part of your task will be to unearth books that are both challenging and suitable. Time and again I have found that choosing the right books is the chief problem confronting parents; and teachers are always looking for fresh titles, carefully selected to absorb and delight advanced readers.

Careful juxtaposition of books is an important part of an open approach, so that the child reads, thinks and compares without being prompted. You will find this enhances book-experience. And book-experience is vicarious life-experience.

Personality and role-modelling also govern how a child relates to books. These factors will determine how much time a child freely gives to reading, the books they choose and whether they want to discuss them.

Eight is an age at which children often take a step up in independence. Children may suddenly start hiding away with books and not talking about them, which may be a bid for freedom and a sign of growing independence. Yet it is wise to know that this sort of leisure reading can be a refuge from pressures elsewhere. The 'solitary reader' is probably best left alone. Your task at this stage is to provide the very best books and have read them yourself!

Responding

Let's look at how advanced readers may respond to their books and how they can be encouraged to let an adult in on their views.

Spontaneous response

The first and best reaction is the spontaneous response of the child in speech.

At home you may be privileged to hear comment that frequently goes beyond mere like or dislike to reveal fuller appreciation or condemnation, but wait, don't ask. Reaction may not be immediate, because we all need time to think. More often than not, questions or 'matters arising' will be aimed at Mum when she's busy cooking or at Dad when he's trying to read the paper. Parents, for instance, should not be surprised if it all comes to the surface when they have just popped up to quickly say goodnight to their young son. Likewise, they should be prepared to spend time hearing (in detail, at some length, and possibly without a chance to comment) their older daughter's thoughts on a book being studied in class. Chances are she has disagreed with or gone beyond what the teacher said, and has not had an opportunity to air her views.

Spontaneous response in the classroom is tricky. The gifted child is often more than ready to contribute to discussion but will either dominate the session or decide to tone down their response to avoid peer pressure later. Writing is safer, they decide.

Teachers then need to allow for spontaneity in writing by avoiding over-prescriptive assignments. For instance, if prose is what you have envisaged will you accept a poem?

Elicited response

How do we find out what has been gained from silent reading when nothing is forthcoming?

It is important to realize that knowledge that comes our way in a life-long engagement with reading is not simply something to add to our stock of information (facts). It is there to be assimilated, to modify our present way of thinking, and potentially to change our attitudes and opinions. Yet we adults tend to get all worked up about whether children understand what they have read. We want to find out how well they remember what the book was about, how much meaning they have taken in and whether their writing will benefit.

A teacher acting as mentor needs to tread delicately. Being there to share is far better than probing. My belief is that to hear how a book has set a child thinking, you need to invite rather than insist. (There is more on this in Chapter 3.) As a parent, you could offer to have a particular title you and your child each read privately and later discuss. But first let's take a look at more usual methods of gauging understanding.

Comprehension

In school, the skill of 'reading with comprehension' is usually tested through questions and set tasks. There is a recognized system in place that

- helps to cope with numbers and a wide range of ability in class
- allows for keeping a record of each child's progress (in relation to expected levels of progress as determined by the curriculum).

In the context of comprehension testing, children are taught to answer questions with expected answers; to practise thinking and speaking skills in discussion; and to do creative writing that will indicate what they have gained from a specific reading assignment.

This can be a trial for a gifted child working within a large group.

Let me describe to you what might happen in a classroom.

COMPREHENSION TESTING – A HYPOTHETICAL CASE

A story or passage has been read by or to the class. The teacher rightly wishes to know how much meaning has been absorbed. The teacher prompts an initial response at a level gauged to give any and every child a chance. Question: *What was the name of the boy in the story?* There is the possibility of a wrong answer, but the hope is that this question is so easy no one will fall down on it (thereby increasing their sense of failure). Everyone should be able to succeed. Yet the fact remains that there is only one right answer. Therefore some children could feel frustrated. They would like to show how well they understood the passage; they need freedom and scope to do this; they need opportunity, and an assurance that what they say will be heard, considered and valued. Success for the more perceptive requires a greater challenge. Well, maybe there *is* a little opening for the able child? There could be an extra mark for mentioning that the boy in the story also had a nickname.

The gifted child will at this stage probably need to be given scope to expand on the single answer *spontaneously* to say, for example:

- how the boy came by his nickname
- who usually called him that and why
- who addressed him by his proper name
- how he (the boy in the story) felt about all this
- how the pupil feels about nicknames (and why).

In a normal classroom situation with children of equal age but unequal ability the teacher might follow with discussion on the topics just listed, at a level rightly geared to benefit the majority and motivate those who need it. Would the gifted child dare 'take the stage'?

Creative writing to gauge individual response could be suggested as an exercise, maybe towards the end of the time designated for literacy studies. Whether this will help the gifted child will depend on whether the teacher has decided beforehand what the outcome should be or has planned for differentiation of outcome.

Meanwhile the child who has finished the reading assignment in record time and (without prompting) probed it in depth

- wants to tell someone what thoughts arose while reading
- wants to write a poem about a guinea-pig with a highly unusual name (And incidentally recommend two books about guinea-pigs that s/he found in the library, one by Dick King-Smith about how to look after guinea-pigs as pets, and the other by Lynne Reid Banks, written as the diary of an escapist guinea-pig called Houdini – and why the name… And how the second title led to reading *The Indian in the Cupboard* by the same author. And that s/he loved it but Mum didn't… And the name of the boy in *that* story… And how he was a bit like the boy in today's reading assignment because he had a nickname, only in this case he liked it…)
- and finally wants to ask if the teacher ever had a nickname when *she* was young!

True, answering questions and writing to order are necessary skills in our society. Formal education teaches children these disciplines, needed for tests and examinations in and beyond their schooldays. Gifted children may in time have to study 'examination technique' to gain qualifications, but ought meanwhile to be allowed to pursue a train of thought, and comment or question at their own level, otherwise they may suffer through being under-stimulated and unable to use the free-thinking gift they have.

An open approach

What all this amounts to is that, gifted children have powers of understanding and deduction such that they deserve:

- not to be talked down to
- to be given something they can readily apply to their busy, thinking lives
- to be given something to move them on in their understanding
- to be allowed to express themselves freely.

Listening carefully to their reading and responding preferences is a great first step on the way to achieving this.

Resource 2.1 Reading Involvement Checklist (Age 5 at School)

[Questions to be asked before the checklist]

What book are you reading right now?

Did you choose it?

If not, who did?

Do you like it or don't you?

What kinds of books do you usually choose?

Checklist

There are several ways of reading. Tick which you do and put 2 ticks (or more) for the ones you specially enjoy:

I like someone to read to me

I like someone to share a book with me

I like to read aloud with someone listening

I like to read aloud to myself

I like to read to myself silently

[Further question, deliberately placed after the checklist]

Which would you say was your 'best book ever'?

Resource 2.2 Home Reading Questionnaire (Ages 4–5)

For the pupil and parent to answer...

Name _ _ _ _ _ _ _ _ _ _ _ _ _ _ _ _ _   Age _

Address _

Phone _

What book are you reading at the moment?

Its name _

The person who wrote it _

What is it about? _

Did you choose it? _

If not, who did? _

EITHER What do you like about it? _

OR If you do not like it, can you say why? _ _ _ _ _ _ _ _ _ _ _ _ _ _ _ _ _ _

What do you enjoy reading about? _

What writing do you do? _

Which have been your favourite books so far?* _ _ _ _ _ _ _ _ _ _ _ _ _ _ _

Is there anything else you wish to tell us? _ _ _ _ _ _ _ _ _ _ _ _ _ _ _ _ _

Signed _ _ _ _ _ _ _ _ _ _ _ _ _ _ _ _ _   Date _ _ _ _ _ _ _ _ _ _ _ _ _ _ _ _

* If showing to a mentor or keeping records parents should add code!

If the book was read aloud to your child before s/he could read, put (AB) after it.

If s/he read it aloud with some help, put (SR) for Shared Reading.

If s/he read the book without help, but aloud, put (AA).

If s/he read it alone, put (AS) for Alone Silently.

If s/he had the book read aloud AFTER s/he could read – or heard it on an audiotape – put (L) for Listened.

This code is useful anyway in assessing the stage a child is at.

Resource 2.3 Oral Reading Questionnaire (Ages 7–8)

Name _ _ _ _ _ _ _ _ _ _ _ _ _ _ _ _ _

Part 1

How good are you as a reader? How do you know?

What was the last book you read?

Did you choose to read it? Why did you choose it?

Are you reading a book now?

Do you use the library? What for?

What books have you enjoyed at school?

What was the best book you ever read in your life?

Last week did you read or watch television more?

If you like a book, do you go looking for more by the same writer?

Which were your favourite books when you were younger?

Do you ever read aloud to a younger child?

What age is the child and what books do you read to him/her?

Do you read any of these? Picture books, comics, magazines or newspapers.

Have you an interest (hobby, sport, art, music) that you like to read about?

Do you like talking about the books you read?

Have you ever wanted a friend to read a book you just enjoyed?

Part 2

Do you like listening to stories read aloud in school, or on tapes?

Do you like to read poems, or hear them?

Have you ever seen a play acted on stage?

Do you ever write for fun and just because you feel like it?

> e-mails
>
> letters
>
> a diary
>
> stories
>
> poems

If you were given just ten minutes in a room with a table and chair, some paper and a pen, and invited to write about anything at all...

> Would you be able to easily?
>
> Would you find it very hard (even impossible)?
>
> What would you write about?
>
> Which would you run out of first, time or ideas?

Do you find it easier to speak your ideas rather than write them down?

. . . .

Last question

Are you happy about (starting a course and) having lots more exciting books to read?

Chapter 3

Openness and Challenge

Nothing worthwhile is learned by compulsion.

John Taylor Gatto (from A Different Kind of Teacher: Solving the Crisis of American Schooling*)*

In this chapter I give more detail on the style and make-up of any Open Way course or program you may create using the essential and optional features outlined in Chapter 1, at the same time stressing the adaptability of my methods and materials, and the overall importance of the basic principles as shown in the Introduction.

I begin by explaining how your course, presented as a new learning opportunity, can meet the needs of a gifted child by providing both 'scope' and 'structure'.

I give practical advice on topics, on Open Challenges, on Teaching Text, and on creating course units for different ages. At the same time, I demonstrate how challenge and openness are built in to every aspect.

Overall challenge: A new learning opportunity

The overall aim is to open a door to a new experience of reading and inspired thinking at a level appropriate to ability. The initial challenge will come through presenting your course as a new learning opportunity.

So what, from the children's point-of-view, will be new and different?

- the idea of making a journey
- the quality and range of books to choose from

- the chance to compare books without being pushed into it (they will automatically compare as they discern what each title contributes to the topic and theme and how fiction and non-fiction complement each other)
- the invitation to think their own thoughts and speak (or write) their own mind
- the freedom from prescription and correction.

Clearly, at the heart of the new opportunity will be the 'reading challenge'.

Reading challenge

This is where you see the importance of the book list, your prime input. The reading challenge comes from the variety of the books chosen for each unit, and the way you juxtapose them around a topic. There are two main aspects to the reading challenge – *scope* and *structure*. By scope I mean a kind of breadth of opportunity. This is what comes with the child's being allowed choice. Choice is built into the nature of the course in two main ways:

- Within each unit the child decides which books to read and in which order.
- The child is then allowed to speak or write freely in response or lead in oral discussion.

Along with this freedom, however, even the most self-motivated child needs 'structure'. By structure I mean a framework that will hold things together, tell the child what pattern of provision to expect, and also allow your course to build. The topics, themes and challenges touched upon in Chapter 1 are the building blocks of each unit and provide this flexible framework, avoiding prescription and fixed outcomes. I will discuss them in turn below.

Topics

The topic you choose will provide the structure for your choice of books. Topics must be inviting and above all must lead to a particular range of books, and this I discuss fully in Chapter 4. The further resources at the end of the book will suggest some more unusual topics you might try.

Younger children will enjoy a wide variety of single-topic units, each offering a mixed diet of books from different genres. Older children may be better able to deal with a unit including more than one topic, linked under a theme. Either way, a topic provides the starting-point for a unit structure that appeals without making pupils feel hemmed in.

Themes

A theme is another way of providing structure, and you can choose one to cover maybe a grade, a year-stage or a chosen period within home-schooling. The theme will allow you to make your course more interesting by linking up topics, and facilitate 'building' as one topic leads subtly to another, despite there being contrast as well (e.g. between serious and humorous poems, between fiction and non-fiction). Children, even the youngest, really enjoy seeing how one topic leads to another and a careful choice of theme can help.

FOR CHILDREN AGED 5–6

Take for instance the basic idea that child and adult are making a figurative journey together, with topics and books as the stages of that journey. An example might be: 'Up and Away' – a 'journey adventure' in a personal hot air balloon. This will make them feel special, as they take off, over the heads of others, not knowing where the adventure will lead. All their single-topic units will be seen as part of their identity as 'an adventurer'. Further Resource 2 Topic 3 discusses the poem that led to this idea.

FOR CHILDREN AGED 7–8

I touched on the usefulness of themes for older children in Chapter 1, mentioning the need to make adjustments in line with the children's increasing maturity. Notice that whatever theme you choose for a year-long course, there is value in continuing the journey idea, for the sake of involvement and continuity. Even if you decide on modules for ages 8 or 9 through to 11, each with its own theme to cover its topics, you can still have an overall theme that covers all modules within a grade or year-stage. Further Resource 4 at the end of the book shows how this can be done.

Meanwhile, a 'journey adventure' theme to follow straight on from 'Up and Away' might be: 'Treasure-seeker' – a year's voyage in a fictitious tall ship called the *Treasure-seeker*, landing on islands, visiting ports and surviving storms, all through the books and topics you provide.

The Treasure-seeker voyage is ideal for guiding children aged 7 to 8 through a valuable time of transition from the 'one-unit-one-topic' stage into the approach that better suits older children. As part of this gradual move into something more mature I recommend an additional feature called 'Notes' that has proved excellent in practice: it means having one extra page at the very end of every unit (after the free space pages), giving additional information about authors, poets and series, or the circumstances in which something came to be written. These pages have proved extremely popular with adults and children alike. A sample page of Notes is given as Resource 3.1 at the end of this chapter.

If you wish, the journey idea can still be part of your course for students of 8 or over. You could adopt the idea of: 'Wayfaring', which is a journey on foot, thus emphasizing independence because it gives the child permission to linger and explore. It will allow you to develop and present your units/modules in line with the way that children over 8 or 9 like to study and learn. The extra freedom involved is vital in maintaining motivation and gives pupils (better called 'students' at this age) more control over their learning.

FOR CHILDREN AGED 9+

Just as I have recommended an additional Notes feature for 7- to 8-year-olds, I would recommend 'Appendices' for students who are aged 9 and above, as an addition to their fiction modules. These could be to cover aspects of story describing what is meant by style, character, storyline, and genre, while allowing what you say to arise naturally from the particular books the child is reading at the time.

An ideal way of doing this is to have a set of six or so where, although each appendix may be inspired by the book list for a particular unit, the appendices complement each other and the whole set can also be read straight through as a single backup provision.

Something similar can be devised for a non-fiction module and presented as a 'Student Reading File' giving general background and additional information. You will find a sample (for age 9) as Further Resource 5 at the end of the book.

Each module of the top of the age-range three mini-modules mentioned in Chapter 4 and outlined in Further Resource 4 can also conclude with brief extra information. The Open Way originals were simply named 'Notes at the Back'. If you decide on an extended reading list to complete the course for that age of child (11+), you can add notes to be read at choice, giving any details you wish.

THE PHILOSOPHY BEHIND THE NOTES AND APPENDICES

Maybe if you are working with a child at home you might find the idea of adding Notes and Appendices unnecessary, or even a little daunting. It was first done for schools, to encourage independent learning and involvement with the course by:

- presenting a grown-up way of doing things – a compliment to the pupils' capabilities (teachers might like to call 9+ pupils 'students' for the same reason)

- presenting something at the end, so that it appears even more optional than the basic Teaching Text and gives further adult-style independence to the more mature pupils/students (the plan also emphasizes the prime importance of the books and the value of students' own reactions to them)

- providing something to follow on to, at the same time encouraging the habit of reading such extras with interest and thought; and possibly inspiring pupils to undertake further research, especially in non-fiction areas.

Simply decide if this style of information-sharing (not teaching!) will fit your case. A parent could instead suggest searching for sources of extra information in a library or on the internet.

Open Challenges

I mentioned in my Preface the way my father ran his schoolroom, following the Parents' National Education Union principles of Charlotte Mason, about whom you can read more in Appendix 1. It seems the basic idea of free response must have stayed with me from those days. Following a reading assignment, children are simply asked to tell an adult what they learned. They may question the adult, but the adult does not ask questions to aid the child's response, the reason being that a question often provides half the answer.

While your free space pages will allow for totally unprompted response when the child is willing, you will be quick to realize that a child familiar with school practice will surely expect questions, most likely of the usual closed kind requiring a specific 'right answer', with the corresponding possibility of getting it wrong.

By contrast an Open Challenge, though admittedly still some kind of prompt, is designed to trigger the use of those all-important, higher-order thinking skills described in the Introduction. Being 'opinion-based' the child's answer cannot then be judged 'right' or 'wrong'.

From the adult point-of-view, Open Challenges prompt valuable feedback from the child, allowing for reinforcement through praise and encouragement (if needed) and incidentally for assessment of the child's progress, if that is needed.

An Open Challenge should:

- invite a response rather than insist on an answer
- allow for a valid personal reaction rather than some answer the child believes is expected
- set value on the child's opinion, powers of analysis and so on, and thus on the child
- encourage greater depth of thought
- lead the child to compare titles and texts without being asked to do so
- draw attention to certain authors, illustrators and series through inviting the child's view of a sample and pointing them towards further titles
- allow for a brief or a fuller answer, without demanding to know why they choose or say as they do, but welcoming that information when it is offered
- invite a child to assess poetry using terms you may have chatted to them about in the Teaching Text; but this is not the same as running through each poem with them and insisting on a specific analysis; and in the end what really counts is whether they say they like the poem or not!

Typical Open Challenges for different age groups:

Ages 4 to 5

- Do you remember which alphabet book you used?

- Which of these poems did you like best?

- Please tell us what you found out.

Ages 5 to 6

- What do you do to be peaceful?

- What is the best thing about the Spring?

- Which book really surprised you?

- Did you find out anything you did not know before?

- Did you have a favourite book this week? Would you like to share it with someone else, or read it again yourself?

- Name any other funny book you have come across.

- Do you like writing?

Ages 7 to 8 and over

- Then the long two days are over at last and you land in a wonderful place. Well? What is it like?

- There are several 'sayings' or 'expressions' in this unit. Had you met them before? Can you quote others?

- Which poem or poems appealed to you?

- What kind of dragon would you be happy to meet?

- Are you good at writing diaries or journals?

- Did you read either of the books by E. Nesbit? Which bits did you enjoy, and which seemed strange?

- When you finish this voyage will you like reading more than you did when you started? And writing, too?

- What do you look forward to most about coming home from your voyage?

Age 9 upwards

- Why does anybody ever set out to explore (instead of staying quietly at home and living a more ordinary life)?

- Explorers: what kind of people are they?

- Have you enjoyed reading about the North of England?

- In your own home area, what past time would you like to visit?

- If you were involved in more time-travel, where would you go, and how?

- In the part of the play that you are looking at this week it seems in one way to make it urgent to sort out everything on earth before it happens; in another way it hardly seems to matter because the earth is going to be smashed to bits very soon. Do you think his followers are right to admire the Master?

- Please record the rest of your reactions, thoughts and opinions using the free pages.

Ages 10 to 11

- Could anyone make up a voyage to a fictitious island nowadays? Think hard and say what modern writers often do instead.

- Could either book have been written if Swift had not started it by writing about Lilliput?

- Were any of the characters and/or situations just too incredible?

- If you're stumped get fresh inspiration from Appendix 2.

- Was the poem like the others you have read by the same poet?

- How would your world be different without the famous person whose life you looked into?

- Is science fiction written to make us think about the future or about the present?

You will soon discover that you can easily formulate such challenges for yourself. Children will begin to respond spontaneously, once it is established that they do not have to aim an answer at the bull's-eye target of another person's expectation!

Teaching Text

It is now time for a closer look at Teaching Text – the other possible component that can be added to your unit if you like the idea and think it is needed. In some circumstances, a simple course including a book list, grouped into topics, themed or not, with Open Challenges and Free Response pages will be enough, and I discuss all situations fully in Chapter 5. However, if you do feel that 'speaking on paper' to a child will add something to your unit, a Teaching Text is a great way of drawing a child in. It should be read at choice and should certainly not come over as a didactic treatise, detailed description or review, but rather as an inviting word or two on the topic and books. It is best thought of as 'chattering to the child' or 'a sharing of enthusiasm in written form'. In tone it says, 'I am sure you will find such-and-such a poem or story fascinating, and enjoy discussing it,' or 'Oh, and by the way, did you know…?'

Teaching Text helps in making the unit child-centred and child-led. It is best included straight after the book list.

In a face-to-face situation with a known child or group, Teaching Text might not be essential but could still be useful in certain circumstances, such as where a child at home wishes to work alone with the unit and show it or discuss it later.

In the context of school it makes it easier for the course, once created, to be run by another person. In many cases a class teacher has handed over the day-to-day running of a course to a teaching assistant, relying on the teaching provided in the Teaching Text. This indicates that schools have recognized its value. It is also the case that teachers can then give their attention to more dependent and less well-motivated learners. Chapter 5 gives more detail on the organization and running of home and school courses.

It should soon prove an easy task to gauge the tone of any Teaching Text you choose to write, matching the course you create. You simply need to use your knowledge of the child and your own enthusiasm for the books and 'speak' in an honest and encouraging way, imparting information in an inviting rather than forceful manner.

Plenty of examples of the tone and level needed for older students can be found within the resources discussed in the end section of the book.

Chapter 1 resources offered you some Teaching Text suitable for age 6. Two more samples appear in the context of two units given as resources at the end of this chapter: a unit on the topic of 'Book Content' for ages 5 to 6 (Resource 3.2); and a complete home-style unit called 'Magic Isle' for ages 7 to 8 (Resource 3.3).

Pupil response – further aspects

Space for answers

For shorter responses, written or dictated, spaces can be slotted in at the point where the child has an immediate response ready. This design will obviously work for home pupils because they have the whole unit to share with a parent or mentor.

For schools, the shorter challenges are, on the whole, better gathered together on one or two special pages per unit, inserted before your free space pages. This is more what schoolchildren will expect, and those pages can be handed in to the mentor if necessary, leaving the pupil with their book list still in front of them to carry on with at home. You will find examples in the resources.

If you feel a pupil could be keen to record a response before finishing all the books or Teaching Text, then suggest turning to the Open Challenge pages sooner and filling in the relevant part right away. The younger the child, the more important it is to allow for an immediate response.

Non-fiction approach: special considerations

FOR THE EARLY YEARS

Non-fiction titles can be chosen to match each unit, while maintaining a balance of genres. Some topics attract predominantly non-fiction and need a story or poem for variety. Where the topic lends itself more to stories or poetry, a couple of non-fiction books will do (a) for contrast and a different angle on the topic, and (b) to suit keen non-fiction readers.

FOR SLIGHTLY OLDER CHILDREN

As recommended and already discussed, you can begin to move towards an overall theme and a modular approach, from age 8 or at the latest from age 9.

At this level, within the overall theme of the sea voyage, fiction and non-fiction can still be interspersed within each unit. Provision for response can be spaces in the text (for home pupils) and generally two Open Challenge pages per unit in the schools' version.

AGES 9 TO 11

If you are catering for age 9+, and have decided to design specific non-fiction modules, adopting an almost adult approach, it is best to look for two or three key books to introduce the overall theme (such as 'Explorers' or 'Inventors and Scientists'). These should ideally be chosen from whatever is in print at the time, because each child may need a copy. Afterwards you need to list as many optional books as possible, to cater for any amount of branching out, side-tracking, or delving deeper into a particular aspect. A number of books now have safe website details to help with further research.

An A to Z file for each child not only helps with personal record-keeping and reporting back to the adult-in-charge, but gives scope for choice. One child's reading and research may result in brief notes which he or she can enjoy filing under topics A through Z, while another's enthusiasm may lead instead to a focus on one or more larger projects, and the child will decide what use to make of the file.

Curiosity leads to motivation. Mentors and pupils alike need to be aware that *we remember best what most interests us*. Let me once more emphasize that the method I have described is intended to lay a foundation for acquiring knowledge, and may lead eventually to going beyond the bounds of what is known and into uncharted areas of research.

The angle of approach just described naturally demands its own special provision for pupils' response within each unit.

- It can be helpful to pupils to have a page where they can record for their own benefit what they have been reading, what they have been looking into, and where they hope to go next. Such notes bring discipline and order into what might otherwise become haphazard.

- Then they may need a sheet on which to share with the mentor their activities and their plans; and they should be invited to share a sheet from their A to Z file if they wish. On no account should anything they show be looked at as 'submitted for correction'!

Adult response

Encouragement

If you have styled your units, and in particular your challenges, as intended, then frankly you will be unable to correct. There will be no 'right' or 'wrong' answers, only choices and opinions.

Let me say here that gifted children are likely to be highly critical of their own performance anyway. Praise and encouragement are not necessarily looked for but are generally welcome and especially important where a child lacks confidence. Be willing to enter into discussion, at the child's invitation. Pointing out something to a child, such as suggesting a sequel to a book they enjoyed, or telling them more about an author or series, thus becomes not a correction but a contribution.

Responding in writing

Bear in mind that any extra information you decide to offer in your response (whether oral or written), like mentioning other books by an author the child has found s/he likes, should be such that children can take notice or not as they wish. Information a school-based mentor supplies in writing can be relayed to parents as well as the child (using for example the Mentor's Reply section of the record sheets given in Chapter 5's resources). Parents are usually pleased to be involved and will generally look for extra books as backup.

The box on p.55 shows a mentor's written reply and, although this one has come through from a distance-learning course where the materials were sent to a child for use at home (for more on distance-learning courses see Appendix 2), I include it here to indicate the style and tone of mentoring, whether oral or written, that you will find follows naturally from the inspiration that Open Challenges give the child.

Depending on whether your course is for your own school or beyond you will either be able to witness progress for yourself or it should earn you a message through the grapevine about enthusiasm for the books, and a verdict that mentoring is valuable.

The joy of the Open Way concept is that it can be applied at whatever level and in whatever situation you find yourself responsible for one or more gifted children. Experience has shown that the open approach can have considerable success and leave both learner and educator with a lasting impression of its intrinsic value.

The tone of response a mentor can adopt

Extract from a response to a child aged 6 embarking on her second Open Way distance-learning course (at home, but alongside full attendance at school). You can relate some of what is said to detail given in Chapter 3 Resource 1.

Page 2

Ah yes! Philippa Pearce. You say that *Minnow on the Say* is very long, but it is pleasant and interesting once you understand why it was chosen. It was chosen

- because it moves at a slow pace, the pace of the canoe and the river, which makes it a gentle, thoughtful, quiet sort of book, and

- because it involves a very important search for treasure which will help save the old house called 'Codlings'. This part is more exciting and you can join in the treasure-hunt yourself by following the clues and seeing if you can guess where the treasure will turn up, *before the characters in the book get the right answer!*

Poetry

Good! I quite agree. Both poems actually rely on the imagination, don't they? 'A Traveller's Tale' was chosen because it is about a voyage and so matches our own voyage on the Treasure-seeker. So does one of the verses about 'My Bike'. All your other answers were right, too.

Page 4

I am really delighted the books proved easy enough to read because of the large print and because they were so interesting. You will be learning a lot about ships and seas on our voyage, just as I promised you last year, and you have made an excellent start.

Words

These go on and on through the whole of your life. Some you tuck away in your memory so that next time you read or hear them you understand what they mean. Others get more firmly fixed in your mind and you find you are able to add them to the list of those you like to use yourself, either for speaking or writing.

Sorry I held you up by forgetting to include your indexed book in time for Unit Two. Here it is!

I'll let you into a secret. I love picture books. That is why I cannot resist putting them in. So glad you enjoyed *Unicorns! Unicorns!*

Thank you so much for sharing with me all your news about the (toy) horses you and your sister had for Christmas, and what names you chose for them and why. I found it very interesting and like to imagine you both playing together.

I loved the pictures, too.

Most of all I like it when you use 'Your Space' because I know you are enjoying doing it, and it tells me that you like writing to me. That is just what I was hoping for when I planned Open Way.

Thank you. Your unit made me very happy.

Best Wishes as always.

Resource 3.1 'Notes' Page: From the Treasure-seeker Voyage (Ages 7–8)

Words

The front end of the ship is the bow and the back end is the stern. When you walk towards the stern you 'go aft' and the opposite is 'going for'ard.'

Facing for'ard, the port side is on your left, and the starboard on your right.

Apostrophes

It seems to be a seaman's habit, this missing out of letters. Even when speaking of 'to windward' (direction the wind is coming from), you pronounce it 'wind'ard'. The opposite, 'leeward' is pronounced 'loo'ard'.

(You sit in the lee of something to get shelter from the wind.)

So function one of the tiny APOSTROPHE is to mark the place where one or more letters have gone missing. You can try some of these on your second Open Challenge page.

More of this later…

The Dewey No. for ships – Try 632.82.

The poem 'Traveller's Tale'. The verses are 'quatrains' (four lines long). Only the second and fourth lines rhyme, and frequently by sound though not by spelling. These are 'homonyms'. And MYSTeries is made to rhyme with SOUTHern SEAS, which is stretching things a little!

The poem 'My Bike' was chosen to link with the maritime theme but also, in another verse, with David in *Minnow on the Say*.

Picture books are included because it is good to learn to 'read pictures'. Sometimes half the story is in the picture. Think of Rupert Bear, or Tintin, or Asterix!

Books move at different speeds. Some are 'fast-paced'. Modern readers tend to expect this. Older books dawdle along at a leisurely pace, and *Minnow on the Say* moves in time with the canoe, giving you time to get to know the characters, and work out where the treasure might be!

Resource 3.2 Sample Teaching Text, Open Challenges and Free Space Pages (Ages 5–6)

[Note to adults: the poetry books referred to here are:

A Spider Bought a Bicycle ed. Michael Rosen ISBN: 9780753410479 also widely available in pbk secondhand

A First Poetry Book by John Foster which has to be found secondhand (2008)]

Topic: What's the book about?

Name _ _ _ _ _ _ _ _ _ _ _ _ _ _ _ _ _ _   Date _ _ _ _ _ _ _ _ _ _ _ _ _ _ _ _ _

Poetry first!

If you look in *A Spider Bought a Bicycle* compiled by Michael Rosen you will find: Two story poems, one funny and one sad.

Next look in *A First Poetry Book* by John Foster and see if you can find a poem called 'Sad…and Glad'.

About stories

Lots of books, especially those written for children, have stories in them. Sometimes it's just one story. Other times the book contains several short stories.

Where do the stories come from? Some have been told for hundreds of years. Or anyone can make up a story for you to read.

So you pick up a book and you look at the names on the cover. One is the name of the author, the person who wrote the book.

Maybe you have read a story by that person already and liked it. And that is why you are now choosing another by the same author.

You know where to look for it in a library because the children's storybooks are arranged in alphabetical order, by the surname of the author.

Example: a book by Shirley Hughes will be under H.

And her books should come further along than those by Michael Hardcastle, for instance.

If you take a book off the shelf and decide you don't want it, then try to put it back in the right place. Why? So that someone else can find the one they are looking for!

Not all picture books are for tiny children. Some are for children as old as 9. Some of the most wonderful stories are in picture books.

Then there are the longer stories. These have anything between five and fifteen chapters and sometimes you cannot read them all at once, except maybe on a wet day in the holidays. So they must be really exciting, and leave you dying to know what happens next.

Inside each story is a world of people (or toys, or animals, or aliens!) Between the first and last pages these have adventures.

When you read or hear their story, you share in the adventure.

Turn to your Book List now and see what stories have been lined up for you to experience.

Picture books

Amazing Grace (Reading Rainbow Book) by Mary Hoffman

Library Lion by Michelle Knudsen and Kevin Hawkes

The Birthday Tree by Paul Fleischman and Barry Root

Longer storybook

How & Why Stories by Martha Hamilton

Library: Any book of stories for 6-year-olds

Information

The other kind of book that many children enjoy is a book that gives you facts. It tells you true things about the world we live in.

There are very many such books these days, especially in schools.

They are full of drawings and often photographs.

Factual books

What the author writes depends on the subject.

The first one on your Book List is by a famous writer of stories, but here he is telling you about his experience with guinea pigs. He kept them as pets for many years. He tells you how to keep them yourself.

I Love Guinea Pigs by Dick King-Smith (Candlewick Press/Walker Books)

Make a note of what you liked about Dick King-Smith's book and get ready to say in WRITE or TELL.

What makes people famous? Think about that.

Then decide if one of these little books about a person's life tells you as much as you wanted to know or still leaves you curious.

> *Dr. Seuss* by Wendy Lynch
>
> *A.A. Milne* by Harriet Castor

You may have known already that A.A. Milne is the author of all the stories and poems about Christopher Robin and Winnie-the-Pooh. The strange thing is that he did not want to be remembered for these children's books. He wrote stuff for grown-ups which he really preferred. But more than 80 years later it is his children's books which people still want to buy and read.

I Spy: An Alphabet in Art devised and selected by Lucy Micklethwait (Collins: I SPY series). Lucy Micklethwait has put together a book of pictures by famous artists and built it around the alphabet. The thing to do with this book is to spot what has to do with each letter, and see which pictures you like.

Maybe there is one artist whose picture or pictures you prefer to all the rest?

Put your favourite FACT BOOK in here:

- -

We do hope you realize that you do not have to read all the books?

And you do not have to read them in the order in which they are given.

It helps if you tick those you have read.

It certainly helps to know how you are enjoying things if you can find plenty to say about what you have read.

Maybe you had trouble getting some of the books. Don't worry!

It often happens. Read whatever you can find.

And you can include any books you have come across yourself.

Like _____

OPEN CHALLENGE PAGE 1: Stories

Name _____   Date _____

Which was the first story you chose, and did you like it? _____

_____

_____

_____

Did you recognize any of the authors?_____

_____

_____

_____

Was there any story you preferred to have read to you, rather than read it yourself?

_____

_____

_____

Which was your favourite in the end? _____

_____

_____

_____

_____

How about the poems? _____

_____

_____

_____

Do you ever make up poems yourself? _____

_____

_____

_____

_____

OPEN CHALLENGE PAGE 2: Information

Name _ _ _ _ _ _ _ _ _ _ _ _ _ _ _ _ _   Date _ _ _ _ _ _ _ _ _ _ _ _ _ _ _ _ _ _ _

Please say which fact book you looked at first _

_ _

_ _

Was it interesting? _

_ _

_ _

Did you learn all you wanted to know about Dr. Seuss or A.A. Milne or was there something else you wanted to ask? _

_ _

_ _

How did the Art Book strike you? _

_ _

_ _

Which was the best out of any you chose yourself? _ _ _ _ _ _ _ _ _ _ _ _ _

_ _

_ _

_ _

_ _

Do you usually choose to read books with information in them? _ _ _ _ _ _ _ _

_ _

_ _

_ _

_ _

What new facts did you learn? _

_ _

_ _

_ _

_ _

FREE SPACE PAGES
Topic: What's the book about?

Name _ _ _ _ _ _ _ _ _ _ _ _ _ _ _ _ _   Date _ _ _ _ _ _ _ _ _ _ _ _ _ _ _ _ _

Tell what you know about stories

_ _

_ _

_ _

_ _

Or what you know about certain authors

_ _

_ _

_ _

_ _

Is there anything you want to say about books in general?

There's so much you could say! You must have learned something from the information books, surely?

Or maybe what you really want to say is about something else entirely?

Then do it!

This space is for that purpose and you can ask for an extra 'Write or Tell' page, too.

_____

_____

_____

_____

_____

_____

_____

_____

_____

Resource 3.3 A Home-Style Unit (Ages 7–8)

Topic: Magic Isle
Theme: Treasure-seeker

Name _ _ _ _ _ _ _ _ _ _ _ _ _ _ _ _   Date _ _ _ _ _ _ _ _ _ _ _ _ _ _ _ _ _ _ _

What do you think is meant by 'magic'?_ _

_ _

_ _

_ _

There could be as many as three definitions in your dictionary, as well as definitions for 'magical' and 'magician'.

There is 'the way something excites your interest', as in the case of a book called 'The Magic of Chess'.

There is 'the granting of wishes', as in fairytales; enter the fairy godmother who can turn a pumpkin into a shining coach for Cinderella! There is also bad, evil or 'black' magic in stories, where princes get turned into frogs and the White Witch of Narnia turns creatures into stone.

Good and bad magic come in the books about Harry Potter, which are popular with many.

Of course there is also the magic of card tricks and conjuring tricks; the white rabbit comes out of the hat, or the lady is sawn in half but comes out unharmed. That sort of magic depends on two things: sleight of hand, and optical illusions. In other words you must move your hands so fast that no one sees, and the trick is to make something appear to happen, when in fact it is not happening. The people watching only *think* they see the lady sawn in two!

Non-fiction

See what book or books you can find about this last kind of magic, the conjuring tricks kind, and tell us what you found.

_____

_____

_____

BUT when the good ship 'Treasure-seeker' has to pull into harbour at the Island of Magic, it is not conjurors the crew expects to see!

Picture book: *The Green Ship* by Quentin Blake. Is this real magic? Or is it the magic of 'Let's pretend'. Even grown-ups join in it seems!

Stories

The Magic Finger by Roald Dahl. Is this magic safe? The owner of the finger finds out that power has to be used responsibly (even if it's only a story).

You push further into the landscape and come to some fields, where you encounter a character who certainly knows how to grant wishes:

The Magic Hare by Lynne Reid Banks

Lynne Reid Banks is an author you will meet again through her classics for older children.

Some more detail about using the apostrophe

About names which end in 's'. You can either put the apostrophe after the name like this:

James' book [the book belonging to James]

OR (especially if someone has asked: 'Whose book is this?')

You could say, 'It's James's.'

When there is more than one person or thing involved (as the owners of something) then you have to put the apostrophe at the end.

The sailors' lives were at risk. (There is more than one sailor.)

Do you remember?

Do you remember a certain King Rollo, a character invented by David McKee?

King Rollo had a Magician. Sometimes when King Rollo wanted the Magician to make things happen by magic, he was told to get on and do things the ordinary way (like learning to tie his shoe-laces, for instance).

But what if you were inside a story and anything could happen?

You sit down by a river and have a picnic. What might it be safe to eat and drink? What might go wrong?

After the picnic you stay around for some magic of the really safe kind, the kind which means 'beauty' and 'fascination'.

Poetry

What poems about magic can you find?

_____

_____

Time to go on board again

'It's high time to get back on board now,' says the captain. 'We don't want to get caught on the island after sunset.'

The thought sends shivers down your spine, and you are only too glad to hurry back to the harbour.

'Thank goodness!' you say to yourself. 'There's the ship! I can't wait to get back on board.'

One of the crew has guessed your thoughts and tells you that last time he came here a trainee magician tried to make the ship invisible.

'It was half gone when we got back to the quay,' he says, 'but luckily the young lady was quite able and willing to put it back.'

Being invisible

This comes into *The Voyage of the Dawn Treader*.

Do you know where, when and how? _____

_____

_____

_____

And speaking of that series, you may find one of these biographical books in The Captain's Library on board your ship.

Non-fiction

A Treasury of Narnia OR *The Land of Narnia: Brian Sibley explores the World of C.S.Lewis* (Collins)

Look out for a map of Narnia and study the illustrations by Pauline Baynes. Are there any photographs? Biographies often give you photographs of people and places, and of important things in the life of the person, which of course includes their writings, and sometimes their sketches.

If you never had it, or have forgotten it, it might be a good idea to read or re-read the little biography called: *Beatrix Potter and Peter Rabbit* by Nicola Savey (Warne) which is put together in precisely this way.

The Old Sea Chest

You thought you had exhausted the contents of this, but someone has restocked it while you were away on the island.

And the first book is much more scary than anything that happened to you!

Read: *Beaver Towers* by Nigel Hinton (Puffin). It is quite long, but by no means as long as some of the books you have been reading lately.

Again: Which part reminds you of the *Dawn Treader*?

_____

_____

_____

There is good magic here, but there is also evil magic, which it is definitely best to leave safely between the covers of the book!

Did you have a favourite character in this story? _ _ _ _ _ _ _ _ _ _ _ _ _ _ _ _ _ _

_ _

_ _

Finally you come to two books which remind you of *The Snowman* by Raymond Briggs.

Why?

First, because the magic is gentle and all to do with imagination and having wishes fulfilled. Second, because the words are either invisible or have been magicked away!

Up and Up by Shirley Hughes

and

Sidewalk Circus by Paul Fleischman

Now its time for your Free Space…

Chapter 4

Choosing and Juxtaposing the Books

The only vital method of education appears to be that children should read worthy books, many worthy books.

Charlotte Mason 1842–1923

In this chapter I will explain how you go about constructing your list – how to select books, how to choose suitable topics for a unit and how to fill out the unit with reading material on that particular topic from different genres. I will talk a little about each of the main genres – stories, poetry, plays and non-fiction – and a little about publishers, authors and illustrators.

Books and topics

In the spirit of the Charlotte Mason quote above, it is the books that are the real teachers in this course. The mentor simply accompanies the pupil on a journey through literature and language. Every unit should therefore begin with its book list, and pupils' responses should always be first and foremost to the books.

Selecting books

So how do you go about selecting the books for a book list? Here are some things you need to think about when selecting from whatever books are available to you:

- *Enough books* – 'Enough' does not mean just 'a quantity'. It means also 'a sufficient range' so that there is variety and contrast. A wide range of books, held together by a topic, provides a structure that allows for freedom. It also gives you established points of reference for discussion.

- *The right books* – What do I mean by 'right'? Well, first the books must obviously relate in some way or other to the chosen topic, module or theme. Second, care must be taken that the content is enjoyable, and suitable, for the child's years and experience. Include 'easy-reads' if they can give an angle on the topic.

- *Whole books* – Children deserve these, as a compliment to their reading powers. Once we begin to pick out extracts, or limit children to one or two texts, it is like dictating to them, and we are back with an atmosphere of prescription and compulsion.

You will find various recommendations in this chapter, and more suggestions in Resource 4.3.

Choosing topics

Topic and book choices are inseparable. Topics are also in a sense the 'bait'. Those for single-topic units (up to the age of 7 or 8) are chosen for their appeal, novelty and variety. Over the space of a year, you can touch, for example, on: creatures of all kinds; story styles; funny poems; night-time themes; audio recordings and television; times past; the sea; adventure; fantasy; and so on. You will find ideas for possible topics in the resources at the end of this chapter and also at the end of the book.

Topics 'contain' the books, providing a framework that maintains a balance between genres. The focus can vary to cater for everyone's reading preference. Those who regularly read stories only, or predominantly non-fiction, can be encouraged (not forced) to sample books they might not otherwise go for.

Children will look to see how each book relates to the topic and to the other books chosen. For instance, they will very happily compare the various poems you point them to: about bears, or the sea, or school, or days gone by. You will see from the lists given that some whole topics can be poetry-based with stories, non-fiction books or plays in a supporting role.

Choosing a range of books to suit the age and maturity of your child may still sound a daunting task, but so long as you focus on the topic and on *variety* you cannot fail to come up with a good package.

Selecting by genre

Where each unit has its topic aim for a balance of genres and your range can include:

- stories

- poetry

- non-fiction

- plays (maybe).

It then helps to look for a spread *within* each genre. I will say a little bit about each of the genres below.

Stories

If story is to be your main ingredient, then put in a good sprinkling. Try including stories that are easy but delightful, with others that are challenging but worthwhile. Examples might be:

- a picture book that is beautiful
- an 'easy-read' that has a message/makes you laugh
- a play adapted from this or another well-known story (e.g. a fairytale)
- a classic or modern classic
- two by the same author/with the same or a different illustrator
- two from the same series
- a serious tale alongside a funny one
- a story collection or anthology
- a recorded version to encourage listening (optional).

One unit need not have all these, of course, but the possibilities are there. Ultimately it is the topic that gives each book list its *raison d'être*. It's other parameters are what books are available and whatever time allows.

FAIRYTALES

Fairytales and folklore underlie many cultures and much literature. They have very wide appeal, many being initially told to adults. It is important to present them to children in a way that is right for their age.

For ages 5–6 the children's versions of fairytales ought to be their 'good old romantic selves' so that little ones can enjoy being princes and princesses, overcoming giants, and living happily ever after.

For ages 9 and over, children can be introduced to 'scarier' tales (e.g. some Irish folklore) and humorous, modern versions of traditional fairytales. See the box on p.76 for one 9-year-old's reaction to a reworked version of a classic fairytale.

Snow White and the Seven Aliens by Laurence Anholt

It was easy but funny. It was mostly mocking Snow White and the Seven Dwarfs – Snow White's the same – she lives in the castle – but instead of the evil stepmother there's somebody called the Mean Queen who was the lead singer in a band called the Wonderful Wicked Witches. Snow White has a hero called Hank Hunk from Boy Snog – apparently a band. It's supposed to be a send-up of Boyzone (I think!). Anyway Mean Queen has a horrible, huge nose while Snow White has a small nose and is pretty (apparently, anyway, I've not managed to confirm it personally). Unfortunately Snow White's father is a bit of a weed when it comes to Mean Queen. So, after a while Snow White is kicked out by Mean Queen (a proverbial pain in the pants!) and, eventually, Snow White turns up at the Swingin' Spaceship, gets a job and meets the seven aliens. The aliens hear her singing and sign her up for the band. Soon the big concert is due, but Mean Queen gives Snow White stage fright. Then – ah , look, it's Hank Hunk! Hank Hunk snogs Snow White and they all live happily ever after, etc., etc., etc.

The backbone of the story is the same as Snow White and the Seven Dwarfs: it's just tiny details that are different. I think it's more funny strange than funny amusing.

By Oliver Canning (age 9)

Poetry

Poetry suits and challenges children with advanced reading skills and thinking powers. The reason is that poets weigh every word they use. With beauty and economy of language, enhanced by rhythm, the poet can present recognizable ideas and situations in unfamiliar ways that can delight or astound.

Learning through reading, a gifted child may explore beyond what others are capable of or interested in at the same age. Both poetry and plays are vital in giving a deeper understanding and more rounded view, and providing valuable language enrichment. Let me give you an expert's comment on what poetry has to offer to a gifted child. In his book *Challenging the More Able Language User* (NACE/Fulton, 1998) Geoff Dean wrote:

> More able language users should be given the strongest possible introduction to poetry, because it is in the language of poetry that many of them will find enormous pleasure and challenge. If children have already shown an inclination to seek for further meaning in what they read, poetry will serve as an area of literature where they can hone and refine those skills.

POETRY ANTHOLOGIES

Anthologies designed by a publisher 'for children' have poems of many kinds, short or long, easy or hard. Children can experience a wide range of verse, explore the book in spare time, and find their own level. They will soon say what they like!

The old-fashioned nonsense poems of Edward Lear and Lewis Carroll are often chosen. Provide anthologies that will contrast these classics with modern humour. You will find it interesting to observe how each child reacts.

Other anthologies are aimed at a narrower age group or held together by a theme.

- Some work to a message such as the importance of ecology.

- Some came out at the millennium, spanning the previous century.

- One or two have poetry from the Caribbean or other countries that have their own brand of spoken English.

- Some have poems from non-English-speaking cultures – poems that still speak powerfully in translation.

- Some include poems by children, inspiring readers to try their hand at being poets themselves.

Children love to have a whole book of poems to browse through at leisure.

My advice is to decide on a good anthology for each stage of your course, choosing for each unit the poems that best fit its topic and simply giving the page numbers to lead the child to the right place. To extend the range, you can also give page numbers for poems in various other anthologies or collections.

POETRY COLLECTIONS

These will limit you to one poet at a time, of course. Do not hesitate to use any classics you are familiar with. The following old-fashioned collections have proved very valuable:

- Beatrix Potter – for the very young

- A.A. Milne – splendid for the imagination, and marvellous for picking up on the value of rhyme and rhythm

- Robert Louis Stevenson, who tells of steam trains and wooden spades, and the gas lamps we know no more; but also of children at play, and feelings universal to children in any era.

There are excellent collections by well-known poets of today. You will know what is available and popular where you live. For example, as well as her excellent stories, Margaret Mahy's highly amusing verse is well-known far beyond the shores of her native New Zealand. John Agard's poems are Caribbean in flavour and style. Adrian Mitchell, Kit Wright, Brian Patten and Roger McGough (all very well known in the UK) write poems that have universal child-appeal.

Non-fiction

FOR YOUNGER CHILDREN

This simply means finding one or two 'fact books' to fit the topic. It is helpful to provide titles that will lead a child to investigate further. An example of this was given in Chapter 1 for the topic 'Just imagine'.

FOR OLDER CHILDREN

A word more about the non-fiction approach described in Chapter 3.

You will need to search the catalogues of all publishers for the non-fiction children's market and will be at an advantage if you already know the child or children involved and can assess where their interests may lead.

To match the year's theme of 'People' for children aged 10+, try working with the non-fiction topic 'Famous People' (for example 'Inventors and Scientists' or 'Artists and Musicians'). Aside from general texts covering these topics as a whole, look for books or sets of books on famous lives and legacies, from Leonardo da Vinci to Bill Gates, Rembrandt to Warhol, and Bach to Buddy Holly or The Beatles. Children have been fascinated to learn about Darwin and Diane Fossey, Edison and Einstein, the lives of Presidents or the life of UK Prime Minister Winston Churchill.

Each family or school can have fun finding out what is available to buy or borrow in their own country, state, district or area.

Here is a design for the top of the age-range involving three 'mini-modules' and covering a period of let's say four months. Module A can be, for instance, about immigration and emigration and 'The Past', with stories and autobiographies. Module B might cover 'Plays of Today'. Module C can then discuss 'The Future', starting with books about the possible real world of the later 21st century. Plenty of these came out to coincide with the millennium and you can research online what is now available. Then choose exciting sci-fi stories to match.

For the remainder of the 11+ stage (and beyond!) I recommend lengthy book lists covering every type of literature and illustrating a wide range of life-situations.

You can devise a 'route' or a choice of routes to give the study of these titles some kind of structure. Your approach might be:

- based on a particular culture
- multicultural
- theme-based, grouping books by content
- modular, by genre.

Plays

I consider plays to be a special source of challenge and enrichment.

- Plays are hard to get and hard to read. They could be new in terms of experience.

- They are a form of literature, to be studied alongside story, poetry and non-fiction.

- Plays as 'drama' lead naturally into performance, and stand alongside the arts of storytelling and poetry recital.

- Drama links with art, music and dance, all of which can be experienced actively or passively within a culture.

Some publishers have brought out plays, including puppet plays, for classroom use with the youngest children. These tend to be adaptations, often of well-known fairytales. It is useful at any age to have some plays adapted from stories. And you can draw attention to films made from books. Of course, if you can see the play or film in performance that is better still.

Authors and illustrators

Introducing children to particular authors, illustrators and author-illustrators is very exciting and worthwhile. (See Further Resources 2 and 4 at the end of the book.) Picture books are especially lovely, memorable and not to be missed. They are both an essential foundation for a lifetime of reading and an enrichment for all ages. I am in sympathy with Lewis Carroll's Alice when she asks, 'What is the use of a book without pictures?'

Visual learners will relish highly illustrated books. They will think, for instance, about what difference it makes if a well-known classic is re-published with a different illustrator.

I recommend having a picture-based topic for each age-group with maybe a title like 'Don't forget the pictures!' for the younger children.

Choosing age-appropriate titles

Emotionally appropriate titles

Where young children whose reading skills are 'adult' get out of their depth emotionally, boredom or bewilderment may not be the only effects. Some books are just too scary. Children have been known to dive into ghost and time-warp stories that gave them nightmares. The author Ann Pilling admits to feeling ill herself as she wrote the final words of her ghost story *Black Harvest*, about the Irish potato famine. Imagine the effect this book could have on a child!

Be aware, too, that older children, trying to read everything a particular author (maybe one they are excited to have discovered) has written, can easily stumble across a book intended for a teenage readership and find themselves out of their emotional depth. It will pay you to research this area and give guidance.

Culturally appropriate titles

It is also worth being aware that some groups of people will have strong views surrounding certain topics and issues. As a parent, you will know already where you stand, but as a teacher working on a reading list it is worth bearing in mind that:

- some Christians would rather steer clear of a preoccupation with magic
- others are not in tune with dinosaurs, except as fiction, and do not hold that humans are descended from apes
- the topic of pigs may prove unwelcome to those of certain faiths
- some parents take exception to books based on a particular religious message.

Series, sequels and popular authors

There are, of course, series in fiction and in non-fiction.

Fiction series can be:

- by author, about a particular character or set of characters
- by publisher (e.g. the Blue, Red and Yellow levels of 'Banana Books' published by Egmont)
- about a popular topic such as animals (horse-riding in particular) or sport.

Many children also want to 'devour' whole sets of books even when those books have a very predictable storyline and are not remarkable for their style. Never mind! The better books will shine by contrast.

Non-fiction series are often published in line with a particular syllabus or government-directed educational curriculum, and tend to cover topics such as:

- nature – insects, snakes, pets, wild animals, the rainforest
- geography – countries, coasts, mountains, rivers and so on (for different ages)
- science – the water-cycle, the human body, food, etc.
- history – toys in the past, periods of social history, especially as they affected children at the time.

The advantage of having predictable non-fiction books on the market is that a book you have your eye on for a unit may be available in school already. The disadvantages are that it may be scheduled for a later year's study, or be aimed at 6-year-olds rather than the 10+ level for whom your module is being designed. The library might rescue home school parents who might otherwise be faced with buying a 'school set'.

But some of the books produced are to a high standard with photographs and diagrams and should definitely not be missed. I hope also that you will be able to get hold of some of the charming biographies of authors that have been brought out to run alongside early fiction and will encourage even the youngest children to dream of being authors themselves.

Some of the books children devour at a particular age will be left behind.

Others, including picture and poetry books, they will re-read many times. Some will doubtless have precious memories for their owners and will be read to or bought for the next generation and beyond!

Resource 4.1 Topic Lists (up to Age 7)

Age 5 to 6

1   Beginning
    Part 1. So you're an OWL! Part 2. Alphabet News

2   What's the book about?
    Stories or information?

3   Does it rhyme?
    Part 1. Sometimes Part 2. Sounds, sense and stories

4   Don't forget the pictures!
    Storytelling pictures and Illustrations

5   Toys and games
    Toys alone and toys with children

'CHOICES' to follow:

Let's Pretend: Bears!;   All Kinds of People;

Pets: Could you Love a crocodile?;   Awake at Night;

Reading, Listening and Watching;   Spring-time and Running Wild;

In Sun, Wind and Rain;   Smile, Please!;

Amazing Adventures;   Tales Old and New;

Summer Days.

Age 6 to 7

1. Just imagine!
   A starting unit. Wild animals, ordinary people, and finally extraordinary everything!

2. Famous authors
   Some we can think of; some you have chosen

3. Pets and their people
   Part 1. Who rules? Part 2. Rescued!

4. Rhyme-time
   Introducing *Four o'Clock Friday* by John Foster
   Part 1. Seriously! Part 2. Now for a laugh

5. A trip into the past
   Famous women and famous men

Extras

As well as reading: Relaxing; Make and Do

CHOICES to follow:

Dinosaurs and all that AND Our world	Story, non-fiction and poems
What's in a poem? AND 'Once Upon a Time' plays	Poetry and drama
Books are forever AND School stories	Focus on reading
Aliens and ghosts AND Does it hurt to laugh?	Fantasy and humour
We'll sail away... AND Down to earth	Story, non-fiction and poems

Resource 4.2 'Fiction–Story': Sample Starting Book List (Ages 8–9+)

[This unit is shown as far as the end of the Teaching Text for Unit 1, which reveals the 'topic contrast' between the books in Unit 1 and the links each provides to either Unit 2 or Unit 3.]

Instructions to pupil: Do Unit 1 then you may choose whether to move on to Unit 2 or Unit 3 next.

Pupil book list

Unit 1   Part 1. *The Dancing Bear* by Michael Morpurgo

Part 2. *Meet Me by the Steelmen* by Theresa Tomlinson

Unit 2 (following Unit 1 Part 1)

The Butterfly Lion by Michael Morpurgo and

Heidi by Johanna Spyri

Unit 3 (following Unit 1 Part 2)

Night of the Red Devil by Theresa Tomlinson and

Tom's Midnight Garden by Philippa Pearce

Extra books to read at any time

The Wreck of the Zanzibar by Michael Morpurgo

Treasures of the Snow by Patricia St. John

Scavenger Boy and *Errand Lass* by Theresa Tomlinson

Unit 1

Part 1. *The Dancing Bear* by Michael Morpurgo

Sorry to start you on a sad note. Quite a few of Michael Morpurgo's books do have rather sad endings and all of them make you think, as you may know if you have met other books by this author.

The Dancing Bear is certainly thought-provoking and the ending is hard to swallow.

We advise having a box of tissues handy before you get to the end. We'll leave you free to say why in your own words. (Make sure you know the meaning of the word *contrast*, as it is a key word for the whole of this module.) For example the two books in this unit were originally chosen for contrast between serious and funny. (The funny title, *Spacebaby* by Henrietta Branford, went out of print. You might find it in a library or secondhand.) Instead you now move on from Switzerland to a time-warp story.

The Open Challenge page is to challenge you and invite you to give honest opinions.

When you are describing a book, pinning down how you reacted to it, and above all trying to compare it with one or more others, you deserve guidance.

It will help you, whether you are looking at stories by others or writing your own.

Part 2. *Meet Me by the Steelmen* by Theresa Tomlinson

Here is your second book, a complete contrast to the first.

When you have read it you can decide whether to go for Unit 2 or 3.

Theresa Tomlinson's book is about a real place in the present and the past.

In both your books you need to take a magnifying glass to the relationships between people. (What does 'take a magnifying glass to' mean? It means 'look very closely at'. You might also think of the expression 'examine under a microscope' but maybe that is rather too close a look in this case. When you really take a magnifying glass and use it to help read small print, then you are performing this action *literally*. But the same expression in the opening sentence of this paragraph is used *metaphorically*.)

Here are some more examples of metaphors:

> *The sunshine of your smile brightens my life.*

> *Don't monkey around!*

Other important things to think about here are:

- your five senses

- and maybe the sixth sense, too (sometimes called a hunch or an inkling).

For full understanding of all your books you need to remember particularly the sense of touch.

You need to think about feelings (emotions) in general.

Your Open Challenge page follows…

Resource 4.3 Finding the Right Reading Material(Advice to Adults)

Some book suggestions

Picture books for young children

with no text

The Sidewalk Circus by Paul Fleischman

The Snowman by Raymond Briggs

with text

The Animal Hedge by *Paul Fleischman*

The Elephant's Pillow: A Chinese Bedtime Story by Diana Reynolds Roome

The Mousehole Cat by Antonia Barber

Fiction for older children

Classics authors

Susan Coolidge (e.g. *What Katy Did* and other books in the 'Katy' series)

Lucy Maud Montgomery (*Anne of Green Gables*)

Rudyard Kipling (*Jungle Book*)

Jack London (*White Fang* and *Call of the Wild*)

E. Nesbit (*Five Children and It* and *The Railway Children*)

Anna Sewell (*Black Beauty*)

Mark Twain (e.g. *The Adventures of Tom Sawyer* and *The Prince and the Pauper*)

Modern classics authors

Sheila Burnford (*The Incredible Journey*)

Roald Dahl (e.g. *The Magic Finger* and *The BFG*)

Dick King-Smith (e.g. *The Sheep-pig*)

Madeleine L'Engle (*A Wrinkle in Time* and *Meet the Austins*)

Elyne Mitchell (*The Silver Brumby*)

Philippa Pearce (*Tom's Midnight Garden*)

Popular fiction authors

Sharon Creech (e.g. *Love That Dog* (8+))

Paula Danziger (e.g. *Longer Letter Later* (11))

Kate DiCamillo (e.g. *Because of Winn-Dixie* (9+))

Anne Fine (e.g. *Press Play* (5–8))

Paul Fleischman (his picture books, especially *Weslandia*)

Carol Gorman (stories for top age-range about a character called Dork)

Anthony Horowitz (*The Falcon's Malteser* and (historical) *The Devil and His Boy*)

Margaret Mahy (super books from very young to late teenage; choose carefully)

Michael Morpurgo (e.g. *A Twist of Gold* and many others)

Jacqueline Wilson (e.g. *Secrets*)

More recommendations from around the world

Land of the Long White Cloud by Kiri te Kanawa (Maori legends retold by the world-renowned New Zealand opera singer)

The Kite Rider by Geraldine McCaughrean (11–12) (set in 13th-century China)

Seasons of Splendour by Madhur Jaffrey (8+) (myths and legends of India)

Out of India by Jamila Gavin (a memoir of an Indian childhood)

Chandra by Frances Mary Hendry (11–12) (a girl's experience of arranged marriage in India)

Plays

Sacred Earth Dramas, nine legend-based plays about preserving the planet, written by young people all around the world

Poetry

Dark as a Midnight Dream (Evans Brothers)

One Hundred Years of Poetry for Children (Oxford University Press)

Useful websites

www.christchurchcitylibraries.com/kids/childrensauthors/list.asp

Interviews with New Zealand children's authors, e.g. Margaret Mahy (some teenage here), Lynley Dodd (youngest readers)

www.barefootbooks.com

For poems about nature, some in translation

www.barnowlbooks.com

Classic children's books lovingly reprinted for a new generation

www.candlewick.com

Children's book publishers

www.childlit.org.za

Children's literature in South Africa

www.janenissenbooks.co.uk

Bringing children's classic books back into print

www.samuelfrench.com or www.samuelfrench-london.co.uk

Samuel French publishes plays for performance – you can get advice from Customer Services on one-act plays for your topic and age range

www.walkerbooks.co.uk

Children's book publishers

Chapter 5

Practical Issues

The proof of the pudding is in the eating.

Proverb

This chapter is about the logistics of setting up a course. In it I give practical advice on the organization and running of a course, whether it be a school-run course or a parent-run course.

School-run courses

The launch of a course needs an enthusiastic principal or head teacher behind it. After all, a course designed for advanced readers is not suitable for a whole-class approach, because:

- it relies on reading ability considerably above the norm
- its Teaching Text and challenges are aimed at quick-thinking pupils
- the range of books it requires prohibits buying in quantity.

In the quote below you can see the potential for success described by Clare Tomlinson, a teacher who has run an Open Way course for several years and in 2003 used her initial experience with the age-group 7 to 8 as the basis for an MA assignment. Notice that she refers to the course as 'an intervention strategy' for a chosen few, which can nevertheless create a learning atmosphere helpful to the whole class. This is what experts have predicted will happen as teachers begin to realize what an open approach can achieve.

> By using the following qualitative research methods: pupil interview, class teacher interview, pupil questionnaire and my own observations, I have found the course to develop all of the thinking skills and to challenge the learner into reflecting upon what

they have read. It has proved to encourage the children to think, speculate, hypothesise, discover, reflect, generalise, synthesise, classify and evaluate.

It promotes the use of inference, author style and genre recognition at an early age and above all fosters a love of books. The gifted and talented pupils (aged 7 to 8) are literate fluent readers who excel beyond their peers. These children were previously becoming disillusioned on a school reading scheme that they considered to be too easy and predictable.

The children have demonstrated that they have a greater linguistic resourcefulness and imaginative versatility in subsequent pieces of extended writing.

The feedback from the pupils has shown that they feel the most important development to have been the progress made in speaking and listening.

[The course] is a small intervention strategy which if used correctly can yield good results. Small changes in individual classrooms can result in wider opportunities and raised standards for all.

Groups, not individuals

It is worth noting that my schools courses, when bought into centrally (i.e. for a number of schools in the same area), were invariably run with very small groups, one for each year-stage or grade. Six to a group has generally proved to be too many; three is probably the ideal number, possibly four. It will be noted that this means catering for less than the 10 per cent of more able pupils for whom schools are often recommended to make additional provisions. We are talking here of those few who most need an immediate fresh challenge. The group size clearly has to be small, then, if these pupils are to benefit and the program is to be manageable. Schools have found that:

- a group in a given year can be arranged to include one very gifted child along with two, possibly three, who qualify as 'advanced readers' by being, say, two years ahead of their peers

- a group of three keen pupils can be expanded to take in a fourth who is currently underachieving

- motivation is higher when children are in a group, because of a sense of privilege at being chosen, a sense of 'being in it together'; and they enjoy having the opportunity to discuss

- peer pressure from those not chosen for the group can be met with solidarity

- last but not least, enough books for so few children can be bought within the budget!

As a one-pupil initiative

Some schools have tried providing for one child only, but studying on your own in school is no fun, and tends to invite trouble from peers. In more than one school, a child initially worked happily with a course appropriate in content, level and style, but when it came to deciding on a further stage opted out. One child was specific about the bullying. I soon started recommending the small group plan as the proper way forward for any school.

Responsibility

No matter whose idea it is to implement a course, naturally the person in charge of the school has to authorize and take responsibility for introducing something aimed specifically at gifted children and will ultimately be answerable for its success. He or she can then delegate to another member of staff decisions about which children to choose, and when and where the group will meet.

Because a 'whole book' approach works best if given its own time, experience has shown that the children are better off meeting outside of class. Some schools have decided on a lunch-hour club. Some have worked with a teaching assistant in the school library or wherever a separate space can be found. Having a teaching assistant as mentor works really well, but the assistant still informs the class teacher about progress and a report goes back to the one with overall responsibility.

Once a course has been decided upon then others on the staff will very likely have to co-operate and give time. Strangely, the busiest schools have always managed best. I guess enthusiasm oiled the wheels!

Basic provision and course style

Regardless of whether your course is

- for one group only (probably run by yourself)
- for others within your school to run
- for several schools in your area
- for schools in general,

minimum provision entails choosing special books for your advanced readers. Next you should make arrangements for these books to be read *by topic*, with an eye to variety, as explained in the section on providing book lists in Chapter 4.

If your route is to be open discussion, with yourself or another person as mentor, you should be certain to follow these guidelines:

- try not to 'lead' or you will destroy the free response element
- decide how you will provide encouragement
- devise a way of recording progress.

Some useful forms for recording progress in this way are given as resources at the end of this chapter. If you cannot spare time for lengthy discussion and mentoring then try to set aside a portion of time for brief oral feedback from the children. Be sure to keep an open approach to challenge and response, as discussed in Chapter 3.

For a full course, you need to decide whether to:

- have a Teaching Text to put the pupils' learning more into their own hands
- go for written challenge and response.

Buying books and budgeting

Books are bound to be your chief expense, because of the need for whole books, good books, and a wide variety for each topic. You will naturally wish to buy your titles to match your course and run with them for as long as the books hold together. Be sure to buy as soon as you have made your list. In other words, be sure of having every book you need for each particular stage of the course you are implementing, and the right number of copies for use with a group, unless sharing around is an option.

There will be titles where one copy will be needed for each child, for instance:

- reference books, like a dictionary, thesaurus or atlas
- your chief poetry anthology
- key books used to start off a fiction module
- key books to introduce a non-fiction module.

Apart from these you need just enough copies for children to swap and take turns, and if an extra fast reader is kept waiting you could suggest some background reading. School librarians are sometimes unaware that they need to stock more challenging titles for children in a top class and about to move on (say to secondary level). One way to reduce your costs is to persuade your school library to bring in books for advanced as well as reluctant readers!

KNOW YOUR PUBLISHERS

Following on from the specific information at the end of Chapter 4, my advice to both teachers and parents is:

- To help narrow your search, get to know the names of publishers and the kinds of book each specializes in.
- Go for unusual fiction titles from the children's book market, by searching out smaller publishers, or quickly buying the latest prize-winning picture book or tween novel.

I should like to point out that you will soon discover which companies publish certain authors, although some authors have titles with more than one publisher. But every edition of a book has its own unique ISBN. Some publishers have illustrators who work solely for them. You will notice certain author and illustrator partnerships. Some publish across the board, and some focus more on stories, popular series or poetry. Some make classics and modern classics a specialist area. Some, like Candlewick Press in the US or Walker Books in the UK, produce large numbers of picture books, many of them for older readers.

Both fiction and non-fiction publishers can operate a policy of first bringing out hardbacks (expensive) and then paperbacks (cheaper), often one year later.

The hardback title you came across somewhere may be around in cheaper paperback under the same or a different imprint; even by another publisher altogether.

As Bagheera, in Rudyard Kipling's *Jungle Book*, would say, 'Good hunting!'

Resource 4.3 at the end of Chapter 4 should help with your search and further book suggestions crop up in the further resources at the end of the book.

Parent involvement

Today teachers are more conscious that parents know their children. The best scenario is where teacher and parent agree that a child is reading two or three years ahead of the norm and co-operate in meeting the challenge.

Schools that inform parents of a course and involve them find they get help with:

- whatever extra reading the pupil is to do at home

- the recording of responses (if a young child wishes to dictate)

- providing new books (it has happened!)

- getting hold of extra titles from libraries; or buying some secondhand.

Borrowing from libraries and buying secondhand extend the possibilities enormously, making it possible to provide a wider range of books including a number of unusual titles the child or children would not otherwise encounter. Books do eventually disappear from the library shelves but last much longer there than they do in print.

Some information on libraries is appropriate here, as it will be useful to parents supporting a school course, as well as to those who are running a home-based course (see Resource 5.4).

Parent-run courses

If you are a parent looking for a course to run in leisure time, then your search will likely be for:

- general advice on reading matter

- books that are challenging but age-appropriate

- books that will 'hang together'

- something that will encourage thinking more about the books.

What I have said earlier in this chapter about the search for books is for you as much as for school providers, and Resource 4.3 at the end of the previous chapter should help, too. Challenge is nothing without happiness and enjoyment.

Experience has shown that the aspects of the Open Way concept most helpful in a home situation are:

- the whole book approach
- the child's joy at being asked for an honest opinion
- the fun and freedom of responding without necessarily having to write
- the discipline of 'structure without prescription'
- the pleasure and privilege of having an additional mentor besides a parent.

Families often need something during a 'difficult patch'. The right sort of learning program can mean that, in a 'sink or swim' situation, the child does not drown nor the parents go under! A course can increase a child's self-confidence enough to make coping with school easier, if that has been the problem, thus avoiding more drastic solutions, such as changing schools, moving house, or even going to another country!

Keeping down the costs

Some families have worked with a book list only, depending almost entirely on libraries. A further step is to try putting together matching course materials, along the lines described in Chapters 1 and 3.

A mentor is extremely valuable as a support to both child and parent. Maybe you yourself will become a mentor having put together a course that others can also use? Maybe someone else in your situation will use this book to implement a course that you will then use, and that person might act as mentor for your child.

Courses for siblings

If you successfully create a course for your gifted child you can adopt the same approach with your other children.

On two occasions, parents of my existing pupils decided on a rather simpler course to suit a younger brother who was feeling left out. In both cases the boys very quickly became fluent readers and more confident thinkers, making them happier at school and at home.

Another time an older sister, Sarah, got involved and wrote a huge number of poems which the mentor discussed with her in detail. One of her poems from that time is given in Chapter 7. She is now a confident teenager and her poetry-writing is still going strong.

Home-schooling

Some children are educated at home full-time because their parents believe in it. There are gifted pupils who have never been to school.

Some gifted children start school but do not prosper there. I know of one who was profoundly unhappy in school, started home-school at 7, and six years later is well ahead of the standard expected at his age. Here is his verdict on the value of the Open Way course he followed for four years:

Open Way has done a lot for me while I have been Home Educated:

- The set books have been a great help, providing very good quality, safe, reading material that has upped my own standard through providing good examples.

- I have become more able to think for myself, as Open Way taught and encouraged understanding rather than 'robotics', and gave me the chance to find things out for myself.

- I learnt to take pleasure in composition through: the 'enjoyability' of the course; the fact that long written answers were not needed; and the variety of medium (tape, email, written, or scribed) acceptable for responses (so you never get bored).

And, finally, I was given confidence by the positive responses and open-mindedness of the tutor.

One family with a child exhibiting dual exceptionality found that the school system provided for *dis*ability more than for *high* ability. This boy's younger sister also flourished more in the home environment. An Open Way course is a good way of taking the pressure off parents, who might otherwise have to dream up what should be done each day.

Home-school educators might find it useful to work through the following questions:

- Shall I have a course at all?
- Will it be useful to find out what age-appropriate books are around?
- Shall I attempt to introduce topics?
- Shall I adopt the idea of Open Challenges?
- Shall I write any Teaching Text?
- Shall I use tape or CD to make a recording?

Also, if you are thinking of a full-time home course, be sure to check the laws in your country including those on keeping records. You may be asked by inspectors to prove that schooling is taking place, as is the case where a UK child has enrolled for school before deciding in favour of educating at home. Basic record-keeping sheets are given at the end of this chapter. They will prove suitable for younger children's courses and for fiction throughout the age-range. Some variation (such as space to record progress in researching) may prove advisable for older children's non-fiction modules.

FLEXI-SCHOOLING

Flexi-schooling is when a child's education is divided between home and school. It all depends if this is allowed where you live. In this situation parents try to get the best out of having one foot in the system and gaining two or three days off to learn in other more child-led ways. A 'flexi-schooling child' may later move into home-school full-time, and it pays to be aware that such a child may at first react by demanding total freedom, but later find that a framework is helpful.

GROUP LEARNING IN THE CONTEXT OF HOME

Sometimes home educators meet in groups and each parent offers an area of expertise. This could be an ideal situation for an Open Way course, and what I have written about school groups earlier in this chapter could prove relevant.

The advantage is that opinions (also books and costs!) can be shared. I once heard that two families of British 'ex-pats' living in Tanzania educated each other's children on a permanent 'swap' basis!

But when does a group become technically a 'small school' and have to be regulated as such? It is essential you check out in your country, state, district or area what the law states about the size and nature of home-school groups.

Whatever you decide to put together as a result of reading this book, you can be sure that learning *and enjoyment* will follow, not only for your child but also for you!

Resource 5.1 Mentor's Reply

From _____

To _____

About Unit _____

Part _____

Mentor's signature _____ Date _____

Resource 5.2 Mentor's Record Sheet

Date _ _ _ _ _ _ _ _ _ _ _ _ _ _ _ _

Mentor's Name _

Student's Name _

Unit _ _ _ _ _ _ _ _ _ _ _ _ _ _ _ _ _   Tutor Page _ _ _ _ _ _ _ _ _ _ _ _ _ _ _

Reading [range of; choice of ; no. chosen from backup list _ _ _ _ _   Extra _ _]

_ _

_ _

Response [Nature and level of; written, typed, dictated (underline)]

_ _

_ _

Challenges taken up: 100% / selectively / highly selectively

No. of Free Space Pages used _

Additional Comments

Resource 5.3 Mentor's Interim/Final Report

Mentor's Name _____

Student's Name _____ D.o.b. _____

Reading _____

_____

_____

Response _____

_____

_____

Forecast _____

_____

_____

Mentor's signature _____ Date _____

Resource 5.4 About Libraries

Libraries can be tremendously supportive.

If you plan to depend to any extent on borrowed books then you will have to explore the services you have in your area.

First find out:

- your nearest public library (and details of membership)
- your nearest main library for the area, including reference library if possible
- maybe if there is a mobile library service to villages
- the name of a librarian with specialist knowledge of children's books in any of these – make contact and explain your needs.

Next find out

- What system exists for requesting titles not held in, or currently on loan from, your branch.
- Whether children's requests are free or are charged for (and how much!) Some areas will allow free requests for books if required for an educational project, and some libraries will help you find extra titles.
- How much notice to give your (children's or local) librarian for books you need to have at or around the same time. It's best to give them a list and a date.
- When and where there will be a sale of books the library has decided to part with! These are a bargain.

Libraries for schools

Your area may have something like a 'Schools Library Service'. It may be run separately from the public library and schools usually pay into it these days.

Schools can use their area service to ease pressure on the book budget. Or they can involve pupils and parents in borrowing extra titles from the public library.

Parents: some areas make book accessible to home educators, but for a fee.

Points in favour of borrowing

- Titles stay longer on library shelves than they do in print.

- You can get assistance.

- You save pounds! I advise buying only what you really want to keep.

- A title that is unavailable to borrow within your area can be requested from another area (maybe at additional cost).

- If you request an in-print title that is not in stock, especially one that is due to come out shortly, the library should seriously consider adding it to their stock.

Less favourable aspects

- Some smaller libraries have closed.

- Some have limited budgets for new books.

- Some libraries charge a fee for requests (even for children's books). You can challenge this at the highest level if your child's education and wellbeing depend upon getting challenging books (including some by authors considered 'adult', e.g. Gerald Durrell).

NOTE

- Picture books for older children may be in boxes for toddlers, because of size!

- Some authors write across the age-range. Shelves with titles 'alphabetically by author' may have certain titles by a familiar author that are not age-appropriate.

- You can explore stocks on a library computer. In some areas maybe online. Ask!

Help keep your library open!

Chapter 6

Language and Writing

Fancies that broke through language and escaped.

Robert Browning 1812–1889

Understanding the importance of language is essential when educating any child, no less the gifted child who needs language skills sufficient to aid and express their rapid and complex thought processes. In this chapter I explain the importance of this, and then move on to discuss the way language is used in speaking and in writing, outlining the particular difficulties encountered when there is a need to write. I then use some examples to show how language knowledge can be passed on naturally within the Open Way scheme of things. Finally, I discuss the composition and transcription aspects of writing; and explain how reading inspires children to write.

The place of language

In giving children language you are handing them a vehicle for their thoughts and ideas. They will also sense that you are crediting them with powers of understanding and levels of interest that match their reading ability. In the context of the course you create, your task will be to pass on, as the occasion arises, knowledge of and an enthusiasm for the riches of language and the subtlety of words.

Speaking and writing

Naturally, your hope will be that children will begin to use the wider vocabulary they gain through your reading program, and through the love of words you encourage in them.

Rest assured, this will happen as and when the new words they take in passively as *recognizable and understood* are gradually transferred to the 'active' area, where the mind stores words to be used in speaking and writing.

Handwriting

Adults frequently expect children who are advanced readers and fluent speakers to have higher writing standards than they can reach. Such an expectation is both ill-founded and counter-productive, for various reasons:

- Handwriting depends on fine hand-eye co-ordination, a physical skill that may not develop fully until age 10 or later.
- The rules of spelling, grammar and layout make writing burdensome.
- Writing slows the flow of thinking and this needs practice; a young gifted child can find the process highly frustrating.
- To these is added the fear of not 'coming up to scratch'.

What all children need, and reluctant writers in particular, is a fresh basis for confidence. So, make room for speaking as an alternative to writing, and avoid wholesale correction of a child's mechanical errors in any writing; present the child with a fresh version instead.

Let me relay an example to show how such an approach can make all the difference.

A dyspraxic pupil would only read non-fiction, because she found fiction 'frivolous'. Over a number of weeks she read the books the course recommended and sent her mentor long pages on her views, which were very well thought out but presented in poor handwriting with many misspellings, no margins, and so on. Her mentor followed a plan of consistently ignoring all these errors, instead homing in on the excellence of her vocabulary and thought. Comments were limited to areas where the mentor could not quite follow what the child wanted to say. The child would often be sent a typed and fully corrected version of her work so that she could see how well she wrote. The corrections were thus implicit. This child eventually wrote me to say that an essay had won her a prestigious competition! It took one book to convert her to reading fiction. It was the Canadian classic, Sheila Burnford's *Incredible Journey,* which she loved because it was based on a true story.

Language teaching

Rather than introducing children to 'grammar' as a separate subject, use whatever occasions arise to explain how language works. The 'journey through literature', the emphasis on reading – these are the areas that appeal to a pupil the most and must therefore be allowed to carry the 'language aspects'. You should find you have two windows of opportunity, one individual and the other general.

INDIVIDUAL

In the form of 'matters arising', you can invite children in on something they may not have known or noticed before, such as the relationship between words or the history of a word and its meaning. In a face-to-face situation, this is easily done. As a simple reminder about a handful of common spelling mistakes, you and the child can make a decorative 'Spelling Bookmark' out of card.

GENERAL

With the books or topic as the starting-point, you can give interesting 'language facts' in the form of Teaching Text. Children find this approach fun and it inspires them to write.

By this means you will find, for instance, that you can convey to every age group:

- how the words we pick up through reading and listening constitute a 'passive vocabulary'

- how some conscious effort is needed to make these words 'active' in our speaking and writing

- how this is true of any language; a surprising number of gifted pupils have one or both parents from a non-English-speaking culture, and are consequently bi-lingual.

By doing this you will bring the children into contact with their own word-learning process and increase their exposure to words and language as a whole.

Interaction between topic and language

It works well if you take your cue from each topic as you go. Not every topic will offer opportunities for giving information on a point of language, but some seem to lend themselves to this purpose quite naturally. Below I give some examples of topics planned for younger home pupils up to and including age 8 that might work in this way. At the end of the book Further Resources 7 and 8 give a complete course entitled Love of Language for older children.

Gifted under-5s

Children at this age are more interested than many adults imagine, both in looking at words and in considering why we read and write. You can ask what was their favourite alphabet book and why the alphabet is important. They love arranging words by first letter. Give your pupils the alphabet in higher and lower case with the vowels in a different colour, and challenge them to say why 'bit' comes after 'bat'. You will be surprised!

Ages 5 to 6½

Children in this age-group can be offered as many as 18 exciting units, each unit being on a different topic. These units are to be taken one at a time but, if you present them in six sets of three, you will be emphasizing both contrast and continuity. To illustrate, here are suggestions based on the first nine I wrote for families, where I was also mentor and so could assess the full impact.

The first three topics attract all kinds of literature from which children can imbibe good language, adding to their existing knowledge without any pressure.

Take, for instance: 'Creatures'; 'Teddies, Toys and Games'; 'Sun, Wind and Rain'. Exciting poetry study can begin with a look at the rhymes (and spellings!) in 'Us Two' (in *Now We Are Six* by A.A. Milne) and an invitation to spot the mismatch between the 'dragons' in the poem and E.H. Shepard's accompanying illustration!

In addition the alphabet theme that started with the under-5s can be continued and developed. Invite the child to make an alphabetical list, of animals for instance.

The second three topics can be 'Reading and Listening'; 'Reading and Watching'; 'People'. The first two involve lots of opportunity for discussion. 'People', with its potential mix of titles covering anything from anatomy to jobs, will allow you to focus on adjectives. I recommend listing as a shared exercise single-word adjectives in two categories:

- what people look like on the outside
- what they are like inside (personality).

You will very likely hear more from the children than you have thought of yourself!

The third set of three could be: 'Just imagine!'; 'Dinosaurs and All That'; 'Our World'. You have met 'Just Imagine!' in Resource 1.1. Note the use of dictionary involved, as well as the subtle introduction of derivatives. There is a play adaptation of the picture book *Dinosaurs and All That Rubbish* by Michael Foreman, showing the language difference between narrative and dramatic dialogue. At this halfway stage you can introduce a 'self-test' that enables children to show off what they have learned. The test can include working backwards from definitions to exciting words that have occurred in the units so far. Plan answers the first letters of which, read from the top to the bottom of the page, spell 'dinosaur'. Children should find this fun.

Ages 6½ to rising 8

If you go in for the long, sea voyage idea as your overall theme (see Chapter 3), it will pay you to let your gifted child be a solitary, that is a 'privileged', passenger. The voyage in itself, where the child has a telescope, the ship its cat, also its Poetry Corner, Old Sea Chest and (nautical and other) non-fiction in the Captain's Library, will bring language benefits. Your child can be further involved as 'the writer of a journal' (supposed extracts appearing in the Teaching Text that conveys the story of the voyage). This idea carries an implicit invitation to engage in such journal-writing, a useful exercise in first-person narrative.

The overall language enrichment will be huge, owing to the massive appeal of the voyage with all its possibilities, including the excitement of finding treasure before the ship returns home. Opportunities for discussion will occur time and again in relation to the voyage and to the literature and language encountered during the adventure, and you can home in explicitly on points that arise.

LANGUAGE FACTS

The introduction of nautical terms will be the perfect excuse for teaching on the apostrophe, with pupils challenged to say what missing letter(s) it replaces. It is possible to explain 'apostrophe s' and 's apostrophe' with reference to Old English (OE) *cyninges tun* meaning 'the king's village'.

There is scope for bringing in lessons on notorious transcription 'stumbling-blocks' in the field of spelling and punctuation. The infamous 'gh', as in 'thought', was once OE 'h' (pronounced like 'ch' in 'loch') and Caxton brought the 'gh' into English with his printing skills, acquired in Holland.

The chance to illustrate the importance of commas will arise naturally. If you are using the book *Minnow on the Say* by Philippa Pearce (mentioned in Chapter 3 as part of the Treasure-seeker course and chosen for its treasure-seeking theme), you will discover that the clue to the treasure has no commas in it. The heroes find out that commas change the meaning and consequently the direction of their search!

You will find exercises on the use of apostrophes and commas incorporated in Resource 6.1 at the end of this chapter.

Growing into writing

Imagine how children feel when told they are embarking on a challenging reading course with exciting books and may write as much or as little as they wish! Of course, all reading enriches writing. What author does not also read avidly?

- With compulsion removed, some pupils wish to write after all.
- Keen writers are enriched.
- Tentative writers can be inspired.
- Reluctant writers blossom as confidence grows.

While swift but orderly thinking, careful choice of words and a basic sense of good grammar are necessary for clear and persuasive speaking, spelling and punctuation belong only to writing. A run-down of the composition and transcription aspects of writing is given in Resource 6.2.

By all means hope for high standards. Chapter 7 will give you examples of what children can achieve. But let the children decide when and what to write, and let encouragement be your watchword!

Resource 6.1 Language Points (Ages 7–8)

Three examples taken from Treasure-seeker and drawing attention to language points that have arisen during the 'voyage'.

Example A

Which of these nautical terms was new to you?

Hammock

Bridge

Helm

Port

Starboard

Example B

Fun with the apostrophe (a Greek word)

Put in the missing letter or letters in each case:

It's   it____s   You've you ____ve   Let's   let _____s

We're we ___re   They'll they _____ll

Couldn't could n___t   For'ard _____

A really tricky one is the part of old ships called the fo'cs'le you meet in books like pirate tales or *Treasure Island* by R.L. Stevenson. See if you can find out what the full word is:

Example C

Comma magic

Who was 'over the moon' in the first sentence? In the second? And in the third?

1. The cow jumped over the moon, the little dog laughed, and the dish ran away.

2. The cow jumped, over the moon the little dog laughed, and the dish ran away.

3. The cow jumped, over the moon the little dog laughed and the dish ran away.

Resource 6.2 Speaking to Pupils about Writing (Ages 7–8)

Now, about writing......!

Some people love it!

The pleasant part of writing is the inspiration, that is

- the thoughts and ideas and
- the feeling that you have got something really worth sharing with the world.

This is known as the COMPOSITION element.

The hard part comes with:

- Finding paper and something to write with. You may be out of ink, or your pencil might need sharpening!
- Getting aching wrists
- Being slowed down so you forget what you meant to say
- Being afraid you can't spell the exciting words in your mind
- Having to stop and think 'Is it supposed to be a full stop here or a comma?' etc., etc. You may be put off putting in what people say, because of 'speech marks'.

This is the TRANSCRIPTION element.

Persevere!

The famous author Dick King-Smith writes with pen and paper or with one finger on an old-fashioned typewriter!

Chapter 7

Concluding Thoughts

What shelter to grow ripe is ours?
What leisure to grow wise?

Matthew Arnold 1822–1888

A definition of 'teaching' I once heard given by a college lecturer was, 'Teaching is structuring the environment so that learning can take place'. I believe that is what following Open Way principles will enable you to do. My book is there to help you. And while you are catering for our fastest thinkers you may decide to advocate the basic approach to other educators, and/or use it with a wider group of children.

From reading to writing

Whatever is read can inspire writing. As an Open Way mentor I was presented with:

- stories in several chapters by 5-year-old Claire (sadly, too long to be included in this book)
- an audiotape of David's new-found interest in rocks and fossils, inspired by the topic on dinosaurs
- humorous reactions to a non-fiction book on the life of a Roman soldier, dictated by Oliver (whose book review is given in Chapter 4)
- Michael's film script of the final chapter of Dick King-Smith's *Foxbusters*, which we sent to someone in the film industry for a critique; and his preferred ending to Jill Paton Walsh's *The Dolphin Crossing*, which the author said was one of the best she had received!

Naturally space does not allow me to share all these, but I have selected some shorter pieces, chiefly poems, to show the inspiration that children can get from their reading.

The children's voices

Two 6-year-olds found inspiration in the topics and language teaching described in Chapter 6. The 'Ships and Seas' topic with its focus on verbs, gave rise to this lovely poem by Cindayniah:

The Seaside

The sea goes splash,
The sea goes roar,
We wade and look at the sparkle on the waves.

What could be better than to gaze and dream?

One day we'll sit, and then we'll paddle:
Listen to the crash or the roll of the waves.

Water will murmur,
Water will rush.
Children will play, explore, sail.
End of day, water will calm.

One last swim,
One last run,
Time to go.
Tomorrow's another day!

Cindayniah Jane Godfrey

Freya's inspiration came from the slightly earlier study of the alphabet and adjectives. She came up with this:

Adjective ABC

A a	adventurous
B b	bullying
C c	careful
D d	dirty

E e	eager
F f	frightened
G g	gingery
H h	happy
I i	interesting
J j	just
K k	keen
L l	loopy
M m	mucky
N n	naughty
O o	old
P p	plump
Q q	queer
R r	revolting
S s	silly
T t	tiny
U u	ugly
V v	vulnerable
W w	weird
X x	
Y y	yummy
Z z	zany

Freya Clarke-Wooster

Nature, whether experienced directly or through books, often inspires poetry. Lucy, who worked at home with Open Way from 4 through 11, wrote a good deal. She was 12 when she wrote this.

Fire

I flicker and flame
I crackle and roar
I climb so high
I fall so low

I am majestic and servile
I am ruthless, yet a saviour
Men fear me, yet rely on me
I am ever-changing, yet constant
Anything I touch is transformed

Lucy Stewart-Wilson

This next poem shows how William (aged 9), whose disability made the physical task of writing difficult, taught himself to express things succinctly.

The Lammergeier

Breaking the bones of the deceased
Screeching about life's problems
Overflying crevasse-like valleys
The lammergeier
It grabs the prey in its talons
Blood seeps from the subtle wound
He drops the thing spectacularly
Picking up the bones
Soaring up to the clouds amazingly
Dropping the bone to disintegrate
To the nest he departs
To wife and hearth
All for a lammergeier

William Godfrey

Witness the apt choice of verse form and depth of thought and feeling in these next poems by Sarah (9) and Michael (12).

Airshow

At the airshow,
The wind in my hair,
As I look up high
Into the air.

'SU 34 that is!'
Sweeping overhead.

'Love to fly one!'
Daddy said.

The fighter planes
Look very mean,
Hide my face.
I'm going green!

Time for picnic.
Burgers. Yum.
'Ouch! It's hot!'
Burnt my thumb.

More planes.
What a bore!
I'm tired.
There *can't* be *more*!

Time to go.
Been a tiring day…
Another airshow?
NO WAY!

Sarah Machin

Writing in March 2006, Michael explains, 'I wrote this poem in response to the war in Iraq, which history has proven was a bad idea.'

Unanswered Questions

We fight, they fight.
We die, they die.
We want to go home, they want to go home,
Yet we still fight, they still fight.
We still die, they still die.
Why?

We win, they win.
Who wins?
Many of us die, many of them die.
We lose thousands, they lose thousands.
We lost many, but still won.
Why?

Do you win, if thousands were lost?
Do you win, because they lost more?
Do you win because they surrendered first,
Because they ran out of troops?

Or do you both lose?

Michael Thomas

So what should 'education' be?

From time to time someone does draw attention to the dangers of the 'fact-learning process' that so many think of as 'education'. Such a process easily leads to over-specialization and too narrow an outlook. Education is by definition a 'drawing forth' of potential, and should be a preparation for life. Let us give children reading challenges combined with freedom of response. If allowed to choose when and how they write, children are delighted to come out with how they really feel and what they really think. Let us therefore respect their views and encourage them to become careful thinkers, who will grow up to contribute fearlessly and positively to the society in which they live.

What are my hopes for this book?

I hope my principles and materials will find their way into homes and classrooms and open a door for one or more gifted children.

I hope my book will bring encouragement to many struggling parents and over-worked teachers, and through them inspire pupils to give their best.

I hope you, the reader, will be able to structure a whole-book approach and cast yourself in the role of mentor rather than instructor. Both you and they will learn a lot from it.

I hope that a deeper appreciation of gifted children's needs, and a widespread understanding of what my approach can achieve, will lead to a new mindset in the field of education as a whole.

FURTHER RESOURCE 1 Poetry Books and Teaching Text on Language (Age 4)

In this resource I suggest two highly suitable poetry books for younger children, and give Teaching Text samples from three consecutive units, showing how to address under-5s on the subject of 'words'.

Unit 1: Making a Start
POETRY BOOKS

Out and About by Shirley Hughes

When We Were Very Young by A.A. Milne

First let's talk about **words**.

We all use **words**, from the time we start to speak. We pick up words we hear other people use.

We then learn to read, and pick up even more words.

But usually people understand more words than they use.

Every **book** uses **words** and if the writer can make good use of words then people will want to read whatever he or she has written. The book will sell well, too. It will be a success.

Poems use words in a special way. We will start with our two poetry books therefore, and see if you can learn something new.

Please move on now to your first poem

. . . .

Unit 2: Words and Letters

Last time we were looking at **words**.

You understand most of them because you have met them before.

Here are some:

c a t   **c a t c h**   **c a t e r p i l l a r**

Did you read the third word without any trouble? _ _ _ _ _ _ _ _ _ _ _ _ _ _ _

If you had to work out what it said, did you recognize afterwards what it meant? _ _

_ _

Can you read this word?

c a t a m a r a n

[There's a chance to break it down and sound it out] c a ta ma ran

But do you know what a **c a t a m a r a n** is? It is a particular kind of boat.

So we do need letters, and groups of letters, for reading new words.

- -

Unit 3: Reading and Writing

Why do people **read**?

> They read letters and messages.
>
> They read newspapers to find out the news.
>
> They read stories and poems for enjoyment.
>
> They look things up in dictionaries and encyclopedias to find out facts.

Why do people **write**?

So that other people can read, of course!

FURTHER RESOURCE 2 Three Unusual Topics for Younger Children

The first topic is Picture Book Illustrations. It is addressed to the creator of the course, and suggests a sample choice of book titles and three Open Challenges of a kind you might use.

The second topic is Plays from Stories. I give the beginning of my own adaptation of 'Goldilocks and the Three Bears' and then address the children about it, mentioning a matching poetry anthology.

The third is about Looking Closely at Poems. It is addressed entirely to a child.

Topic 1: Picture Book Illustrations (Adult notes with samples)

Find what books you can out of the hundreds available.

Specially recommended (2008) to indicate what kind of book to look for are:

STORIES

> *Moon Jumpers* by Janice May Udry, ill. Maurice Sendak

From US Candlewick Press/UK Walker Books:

> *Cowboy Baby* and *Catch* by author-illustrator Trish Cooke
>
> *Where the Forest Meets the Sea* and others by Jeannie Baker (collages)

Three books by Martin Waddell all with different illustrators:

> *Farmer Duck*, ill. Helen Oxenbury
>
> *Rosie's Babies*, ill. Penny Dale
>
> *The Hollyhock Wall*, ill. Sally Mavor (collages)

NON-FICTION (Many in the READ AND WONDER series)

> *The Emperor's Egg* by Martin Jenkins, ill. Jane Chapman
>
> *The Seahorse* by Chris Butterworth, ill. John Lawrence

Also

The River by Meredith Hooper, ill. Bee Willey

POETRY

Out and About by author-illustrator Shirley Hughes

Typical CHALLENGES

Think whether you enjoyed this, whether you found it clever, funny, beautiful, happy or sad...

and how the pictures helped _

_ _

Did you notice how this artist uses bright colours and simple shapes? _ _ _ _ _ _ _ _

_ _

Which picture did you like the most? _

_ _

The next two books each have just one person who is the author and the illustrator.

Did you like one of these books more than the other? _ _ _ _ _ _ _ _ _ _ _ _ _ _

_ _

. . . .

Topic 2: Plays from Stories (Add a poem or two!)

This is relatively easy with fairytales and folk tales.

Sample of child's unit:

Plays involve action. Here is the start of a play made from the story of

GOLDILOCKS AND THE THREE BEARS

CHARACTERS

Narrator

Father Bear

Mother Bear

Baby Bear

Goldilocks, a little girl

Scene 1 The Bears' cottage. Downstairs

Scene 2 The Bears' bedroom

SCENE 1

The Bears' cottage. Downstairs.

(The stage is set with three chairs – large, medium, and small – and a wooden table laid with three sizes of porridge bowl and matching spoons.

At the back of the stage are: an open door and open window. Behind these is a backcloth on which is painted a wood or forest. There must be space for the actors to walk through the door and behind the window.)

(At the start there is no one on stage. Then the NARRATOR comes in)

NARRATOR   Once upon a time there were three bears…

                 (pauses while the three bears walk on and stand facing the audience)

                 First there was Father Bear.

FATHER BEAR   (in a deep, gruff voice) That's me. (He bows)

NARRATOR	And also Mother Bear.
MOTHER BEAR	*(in a softer voice)* Me. *(She curtsies)*
NARRATOR	And then there was Baby Bear!
BABY BEAR	*(squeakily)* That's me. I'm Baby Bear. I'm the littlest. *(He waves)*
NARRATOR	Every day Father Bear, Mother Bear and Baby Bear had porridge for breakfast…

See if you can imagine how the play might go on

You may decide that Baby Bear likes the idea of going for a walk while the porridge cools. On the other hand he could be naughty and not want to go, shouting 'No! I want my porridge now.' Or he could be tired and yawning. Or he could be stubborn and sulky. You choose.

IMPORTANT NOTE

You are allowed to make a play of this story without getting permission but if the story belongs to an author who is alive, or one that died less than 70 years ago, then you do have to ask if you may adapt it.

Michael Foreman, author of the picture book *Dinosaurs and All That Rubbish* had to agree to let other writers make the play of his book, which you can buy from Samuel French.

You can see that plays are not easy to read, but you can always try.

Matching Poetry Anthology: *Who's Been Sleeping in My Porridge?* by Colin MacNaughton

. . . .

Topic 3: Looking Closely at Poems (unit for child)

Why take a close look at how poetry works?

Why would you want to know?

- Well, it might be *so that you can learn how to write poems yourself*. You may have written some poems already. Keep learning by reading poetry, and keep practising.

- On the other hand, you might not want to write poems.

- In that case, your closer look will simply be to help you understand and better *appreciate* poems of many kinds.

- You will be surprised how having a better understanding makes you enjoy the poem more.

'The Balloon' by John Mole is about the inventor of the hot-air balloon.

[re-published 2007 by Peterloo Poets in *This is the Blackbird* ISBN 9781904324447]

As the balloon rose far above the crowd, the inventor felt that he had 'risen above' the people who had not believed in him or in his idea.

In the poem he says he feels sorry for them, because he has what is called 'the last laugh' (an expression that comes from a proverb: 'He who laughs last, laughs longest').

He knows that he will never be the same again.

He began by dreaming of his invention and now it is real. The last line tells you that he is a changed person by the time he lands.

CHALLENGES

Have you seen a hot-air balloon either on TV or in real life?

How might you have felt if you were the first one up in a hot-air balloon?

Could you write a poem or story about flying?

Do you like the idea of an imaginary 'voyage'? You might come down to earth again feeling good.

Matching stories: Could either be true?

The Boy Who Could Fly by Sally Gardner

Mrs. Cockle's Cat by Philippa Pearce

Further poetry about CHILDHOOD

In *Now We Are Six* by A.A. Milne: 'Binker' and 'Sneezles'

In *The Oxford Treasury of Children's Poems*: 'Bedtime' by Eleanor Farjeon

There are three R's that can be used in poetry:

- **R**hyme. Ask yourself, ' Does this one rhyme?' Take a look at what and where the rhymes are.

- **R**hythm. See if there is a pattern. It could be instead a natural rhythm like the one for thinking or speaking.

- **R**epetition. Poems often have words and even whole lines repeated for effect.

FURTHER RESOURCE 3 An Older Child's Poem with the Mentor's Response (Age 11+)

This is given as a sample of the kind of encouragement an adult can give a child.

This home student surprised everyone with a lovely poem about his dog. The mentor's response reveals to him how his heart inspired him to make right use of techniques.

Calypso

Her loving head under my hand
Is soft and warm.
Her eyes meet mine and shine
Like emerald-gold.

Her warm tongue against my skin
Caresses my face.
I bend to stroke her soft coat
Full of autumn colours.

Excitement becomes hyperactivity
When there's a knock at the door.
She bounces around howling
With her tail cleaning the floor.

Jumping up at the visitor
She licks her in greeting.
Welcoming with kindness
At every new meeting.

Zechariah Rawson-Roberts

Critique of the poem, 'Calypso':

1. Your poem uses rhyme in a way that does not obtrude, and adds to rather than detracts from the meaning. Well done!

2. I like the 'internal rhyme' in line 3 'mine and shine'.

3. In the first two verses there are short, strong words that hit home, emphasizing the strength of the love received and given.

4. I like 'caresses' because while humans do this with their hands, you cleverly apply it to the dog's tongue instead.

5. I like the word 'emerald-gold' and the line 'Full of autumn colours'. It shows great sensitivity.

6. You have used *alliteration* (e.g. lots of words beginning with 'c' in that verse) to great effect.

7. Similarly, you have used *assonance* (bounces around howling).

8. The last two verses are full of words ending in '-ing' and these reflect the 'hyperactivity' as they have more 'bustle' about them, so-to-speak.

To sum up: You have used *sound* and *sense* to great effect. Excellent!

FURTHER RESOURCE 4 Topic and Module Ideas (Ages 7–11)

For the age-range 7–8, referring to the theme of a long sea voyage as discussed in Chapters 3 and 6, I give topic names for units; and some notes.

For the age-range (8)/9/10 I give an outline plan for a year's program divided into three stages/modules: FICTION – STORIES; NON-FICTION; FICTION – POETRY & PLAYS.

For the age-range 9/10 I outline theme and topics for a further year's work on similar lines.

Finally I offer a basic structure for use with age 11.

. . . .

Topic ideas – Ages 7–8

This relates to the voyage in a tall ship (Treasure-seeker) with ports of call (see Chapters 3 and 6), and features

- The Captain's Library (Non-fiction)
- Poetry Corner
- The Old Sea Chest (picture books and easy reads)
- A journal (supposed to be written by the child)
- and various happenings on board or on shore.

Setting Sail	At Sea	The First of the Islands
On Course for Dragon Isle	Back at Sea	Magic Isle (given in full at the end of Chapter 3)
Catport	Gold Island	
Picture Land	On shore with [minibeasts, snakes]	Sea Creatures
The Entertainers (music, dance, drama)		Storms and Horrors
	Slices of Time	A Pleasant Land
On Shore with the Writers	The Return Voyage	Home, Sweet Home.

. . . .

Possible topic variations: It's Raining Cats and Dogs!

Sense and nonsense; Land of Story-books; Moon and Stars; Treasure!

NOTES

1. *The Voyage of the Dawn Treader* by C.S.Lewis can be used as an introduction/background to the whole voyage and the idea of ports of call and islands.

2. There is plenty of material to be found on dragons, including poetry.

3. 'Catport' can include the poem 'Macavity' from *Practical Cats*, T.S. Eliot's title that led to the musical show. It can go ahead into railways (non-fiction) and E. Nesbit's *The Railway Children*, source of more than one film.

4. Michael Morpurgo has written many sea stories. Try for *Kensuke's Kingdom*, his 'Robinson-Crusoe-style' story that has an adaptation.

. . . .

Topic ideas – Ages (8)/9/10
Overall theme: The Earth/Environment
A. Within MODULE: FICTION – STORIES

Unit 1 (* for shorter version see the resources at the end of Chapter 4)

Unit 1 has to be built around between two and four titles (recommended: one by Michael Morpurgo) chosen for contrast, i.e. one for each of the categories for Units 2 to 6, which can then follow in any order, as each child is inspired by the books in Unit 1.

Unit 2 Space theme

Unit 3 (Michael Morpurgo) Alpine theme

Unit 4 Fairytales serious; fairytales humorous

Unit 5 Time travel

Unit 6 Little people (easier titles – e.g *The Minpins* by Roald Dahl, *The Borrowers* by Mary Norton.) NOTE: harder titles are shown below for ages 9/10.

B. Within MODULE: NON-FICTION (See Further Resource 5 for sample Teaching Text)

Main theme for module: Explorers

After reading one or more general books on the topic of Exploration, further optional routes to take might be:

1. The historical angle:

    *   by land
    *   by sea

2. Mountaineering

3. The Poles

4. Under the sea

5. Space

6. Particular continents/countries

C. Within MODULE: FICTION – POETRY & PLAYS

Theme for module: Planet Earth

Topics: Nature; Conservation; Pollution; Legends from various cultures (e.g. creation stories).

Recommended book of plays: *Sacred Earth Dramas* – published by Faber and Faber

. . . .

Topic Ideas – Ages 9/10
Overall theme: People
A. Within MODULE: FICTION – STORIES

Taking one whole unit each time

Theme: People

Unit 1	contrasting titles with a detective theme (Sherlock Holmes; *Emil and the Detectives*)
Unit 2	taking up again the theme of 'little people'(include *Gulliver's Travels* (Lilliput only!), and a sequel, *Mistress Masham's Repose* by T.H. White)

Continue then

'Against a background of the late 19th, 20th and early 21st centuries.'

[Mostly modern titles with subject matter reflecting these times.]

Unit 3   early 20th Century

Unit 4   unusual titles about World War II

Unit 5   the world of the 50s and 60s

Unit 6   later fantasy and humour

B. Within MODULE: NON-FICTION

Main theme: What kind of person?

Famous people, for example Inventors and Scientists; Artists and Musicians

Routes:

1. Study one or more individuals.

2. Take a period of history.

3. Take a topic; invention, science, astronomy, art, music…

C. Within MODULE: FICTION – POETRY & PLAYS

Theme: People

Poetry anthologies with a 'people' focus. Serious and humorous.

Plays with a detective and/or fantasy theme.

· ·

Topic Ideas – Age 11
Overall theme: Life Situations (See Chapter 4)

Future: Non-fiction, Science fiction

Present: Plays

Past: Stories and autobiographies.

Poetry reflecting all three.

Reading List to extend experience of life and literature.

FURTHER RESOURCE 5 Non-fiction Teaching Text (Age 9+)

This relates to the non-fiction module suggested in Further Resource 4.

Students' Reading File for Module: Explorers

HOW TO USE YOUR ATLAS and/or relief maps in books

Maps suited to studying exploration

To understand what was involved in each journey of exploration, you will need 'relief maps'. (Some of the maps you come across may be flat and not show the mountains and plains.)

For this project, then, you will need to look at a map marked 'Physical'. A map marked 'Political' will show you the boundaries of countries (and remember these will be the countries of the 20th/21st centuries, because boundaries and names of countries do change).

A Physical map shows

- the height of the land above sea level, and sometimes below
- how deep the sea is in each area
- rivers, lakes and oceans
- where the world's deserts are to be found.

For the first two of these you need to look at the colour key given you somewhere on the page. As we do not know which book or atlas you are using we can only suggest likely areas that show the biggest contrasts.

Please look for these:

1. Any map that shows the source of the River Nile.

2. A map that shows the Himalayas and Mount Everest, or the Andes. That will show you the colour for the highest mountains.

3. A map of South Africa. That should show you a variety of terrains and four depths of sea.

If you are lucky your atlas will also have special maps and charts showing which way the winds usually blow. This will help you understand the difficulties and hardships faced by seafarers on their voyages of exploration.

We hope these hints will help you imagine the world's great journeys more accurately.

. . . .

Exploration: Questions

Here are some important questions for you to consider.

Why? Well after you have read through your main book and found out more from others you will have gathered a great heap of information about all sorts of times and places and people. After a while it's time to stop and think about something called 'the implications'.

1. Why does anybody ever set out to explore (instead of staying quietly at home and living a more ordinary life)?

2. Explorers: what kind of people are they?

To answer those questions you need to look at the circumstances surrounding each of the exploits you have read about and researched.

Who first got the idea of going somewhere? Who went? For what reasons? Did the person who wanted the exploration done do it themselves, or was it a case of a king or queen appointing someone?

Was anyone forced to go, or were they all ready and willing?

Character: Doubtless you have thought about characters in fiction. Now is your chance to write about real-life characters. You may find them described by someone who knew them, or you may have to judge them by their actions. Pictures? No cameras in the early days, of course, but the rich and famous (or their patrons) had painters to do portraits or engravings.

. . . .

Looking for answers

Why set out to explore?

Here are three possible reasons and it could be useful to see where each of these applies to the journeys and voyages you are learning about.

1. PERSONAL. In some cases an individual person wants to set out to discover something. Whose names will you write under this heading?

2. COMMERCIAL. Here we are talking about TRADE. A country decides it needs a quicker route to another country, by land or by sea, so as to be able to buy and sell goods. We recommend you list these cases, if this aspect is one that interests you. Or you could talk about the leaders of the expeditions; or the routes they either found, or wanted to find but didn't. Sometimes they found another place or route instead.

3. POLITICAL. You can find several examples of competition between countries. In these cases there may be a race

- to find the quicker route

- to find gold

- to find and claim new lands.

Interesting background information

Stanley, the African explorer, would not have been able to do what he did if a rich American had not adopted him at the age of 19 and given him the money for it.

. . . .

What's behind it all?

You have thought about several aspects of exploration. Here are some more.

As time goes by more and better exploration is possible.

- Think about why a voyage with Captain Cook would be safer than a Viking voyage, more efficient, more comfortable.

- Think about inventions that made sailing easier.

- Think about discoveries made on voyages and journeys, discoveries that improved health, or changed the way people looked at the world.

- Think about improvements in craft and manufacture.
- Think about improvements in sending messages.

Pause and think about extra information from other sources

On the internet you can explore

- National Geographic
- The Royal Geographical Society in London

Have you heard of either of these? There are books put together 'in association with' these organizations. Can you find out more?

Some interesting objects are stored at the Royal Geographical Society.

On the very last evening of the 20th century the following were shown on UK TV:

1. the very hats that Stanley and Livingstone were wearing when they met in the middle of Africa!
2. the sextant thought to be used by Captain Cook on his famous voyages.

Easter Island and trees

By the way, the famous naturalist David Attenborough told on TV how he had bought a long, thin, wooden, carved 'head'. There was one like it in Russia, but it did not come from there. Eventually he found out that a young member of Captain Cook's crew had brought it away from Easter Island. This carved head was done in the days when there were still trees on Easter Island. The island has no trees now because at one stage they were all chopped down for fuel.

Trees, incidentally, can live a long time. There is a yew in England that is nearly 900 years old. In Africa and India there are baobab trees, which not only live long but grow in a fascinating way. In North America there are extremely ancient trees. Find out more?

The South Pole

Because of the sub-zero temperatures, the hut where Captain Scott and his team spent the winter over a hundred years ago looks just as it did when they left it. The materials available in those days were not very adequate: tinned food which was lacking in essential vitamins; wool and cotton for clothing; wood and metal for sledges, and so on. Nowadays we understand what is necessary to maintain a healthy diet; we have warm synthetic materials to keep out cold; and there are three flights to the Pole every day!

. . . .

Beneath the waves: above the skies

You have now been an Explorer for some time. Let's put aside roaming the earth and crossing oceans and

- go under the ocean: The ocean is amazing. In the 20th century fishermen found the coelocanth was still alive in the waters around Madagascar, when previously only its fossilized remains had been found. So it was not extinct after all! Look out for any TV programmes about the depths of the ocean and the creatures that until recently no one knew were there.

   Think about how we are now able to explore more of the ocean than our ancestors could.

- go into space: Perhaps you know about some of mankind's ventures in space during the 20th and 21st centuries. Would you like to follow up on this area of discovery? There are many exciting developments. How about prospects for the future?

Final questions to think about

Are there any parts of the Earth left to explore? Are there still jungles to be penetrated? mountains to climb? glaciers to be traversed? deserts to cross?

How about the oceans around the Poles? How about living on Mars?

Your own travels with the famous explorers; how would you record them?

You could join a crew and write your own journal.

You could be a journalist and report an event in your newspaper.

Could you pretend to have taken some modern recording equipment into the past?

Other genres

It is very important not to lose track of other genres while you are studying fact.

How many times have you read a story about some event in history?

If you are a keen writer, then anything and everything you have been reading in the area of non-fiction could inspire you to write fiction! What approach will you take?

A poem?

If someone's life or experience has touched you deeply you may wish to write a poem. A child once wrote a long poem about a Viking on a voyage, with experiences and thoughts, and wondering about the leader and the purpose of the voyage, and longing for home and family.

A film?

You may find it easy to imagine the historical facts as a film. Will you invent characters? Where would you begin and end. You could plan a film and give samples of the script, maybe?

FURTHER RESOURCE 6 New Ideas for Various Ages: Topics and Books

This section offers fresh inspiration and some practical help. First I touch on tying in plays with stories, this time for older children (for younger children see Further Resource 2). I also offer two themes for any age: 'poetry' and ' illustrations'. I then list seven topics that can be further developed according to need, and finally expand with guidance on books (see Chapter 4) and some Teaching Text (see Chapter 3).

First a list of 10 basic ideas for a topic or module.

Older children

1. Tie in stories with plays

Themes for any age

2. Poetry primarily for enjoyment; secondly for shape and meaning
3. Intriguing picture books (study of illustrations in general)

Topics that lend themselves to expansion

4. Story adventure – can lead on to travel, biography and autobiography
5. Nature – guided by the child's interests – starting with non-fiction and moving on to poetry and story
6. Fantasy and imagination
7. A period in history (non-fiction)
8. Historical fiction – following a child's interest in a given time or place
9. Literature against one or more specific cultural background
10. Books *by author* – includes all classics and modern classics

1. Tie in stories with plays

There are plays of:

- some stories by Roald Dahl, e.g. *Fantastic Mr. Fox*
- *The Lion, The Witch and the Wardrobe* and *The Voyage of the Dawn Treader* by C.S. Lewis
- *Haroun and the Sea of Stories* by Salman Rushdie
- *The Granny Project* by Anne Fine
- *The Wind in the Willows* by Kenneth Graham (Play by Alan Bennett, suitable age 11)

2. Poetry: primarily for enjoyment; secondly for shape and meaning

Taking an anthology such as *Dark as a Midnight Dream* compiled by Fiona Waters and published by Evans Brothers, it is easy to pick out poems in categories.

This has been done successfully taking CHILDHOOD, ADULTHOOD & LATER YEARS.

3. Intriguing picture books (also study of illustrations in general)

Fiction

Just a few of the many illustrators and author/illustrators to look out for:

Shirley Hughes	Janet Ahlberg
Quentin Blake	Shoo Rayner
Maurice Sendak	Bob Graham
Edward Ardizzone	Anthony Browne
Colin McNaughton	Brian Wildsmith
Emma Chichester-Clark	Jane Ray
Judith Kerr	Dr. Seuss
Trish Cooke	Helen Oxenbury

Jez Alborough	Jane Chapman
Michael Foreman	Penny Dale
Tony Ross	Christian Birmingham
P.J. Lynch	Nicola Bayley
Charlotte Voake	Sally Mavor
Ruth Brown	AND MANY MORE

Pauline Baynes – best known as illustrator for *The Chronicles of Narnia* by C.S. Lewis

Nick Sharratt – best known as illustrator for Jacqueline Wilson

Inga Moore – including her superbly illustrated edition of *The Wind in the Willows* (Candlewick/Walker – in two volumes or one)

Compare with more recent illustrations of the same classics

Tenniel for Lewis Carroll

E.H. Shepard for A.A. Milne – his originals were line drawings but a colour version is now available; he also illustrated *The Wind in the Willows*

Beatrix Potter – the original water-colour paintings

Arthur Rackham – e.g. Aesop's Fables

Particular titles – from picture-only titles to more advanced text

The Snowman by Raymond Briggs

Up and Up by Shirley Hughes

Where the Forest Meets the Sea and others by Jeannie Baker (collages)

The Patchwork Cat by Nicola Bayley and William Mayne

Moon Jumpers by Janice May Udry, ill. Maurice Sendak

The Mousehole Cat by Antonia Barber and Nicola Bayley

The Minstrel and the Dragon Pup by Rosemary Sutcliff

Ignis by Gina Wilson and P.J. Lynch

Pepi and the Secret Names by Jill Paton Walsh (Frances Lincoln)

Non-fiction

Compare drawings and paintings with maps and photographs. Look at the value of layout in general.

Unusual: *Look and Wonder: Dragons* by Gerald Legg

. . . .

4. Story adventure

This topic is appealing at any age and has all sorts of possibilities.

One way of developing it would be to start from something a child is already reading. Another would be to choose contrasting books: one serious, one funny; one old-fashioned, one modern.

. . . .

5. Nature: maybe with a particular focus such as creatures, or weather, or environment

Stories

These you should have no trouble in finding.

For older children – adult authors Rolf Harris and Gerald Durrell can appeal.

Non-fiction – excellent and unusual books (9–11)

(Australian) *Yellow-Eye* by David Spillman (Era Publications – Ragged Bears Catalogue)

New Animal Discoveries by Ronald Orenstein (Key Porter Books – Ragged Bears Catalogue)

Poetry (10–11)

In The New Faber Book of Children's Verse ed. Matthew Sweeney there are many poems about nature, including several by Ted Hughes…

Also 'Don't Call Alligator' by John Agard

'Sardines' by Spike Milligan

'Toad' by Norman MacCaig

'Burying the Bird' by John Whitworth

'The Runaway' by Robert Frost

'Five Eyes' by Walter de la Mare

'The Hawk' by George Mackay Brown.

6. Fantasy and imagination
Younger children

Titles in all genres abound. Some classics and a great many about time travel. Author examples: Frank.L. Baum, E. Nesbit, Madeleine L'Engle, C.S. Lewis, Mary Norton, Theresa Tomlinson.

POETRY

Crack Another Yolk compiled by John Foster (Oxford)

Older children (9+)

Stories are easy to find.

RECOMMENDED TITLES

Hello! Is Anybody There? by Jostein Gaarder (Bloomsbury)

When Marnie Was There by Joan G. Robinson (Collins)

Momo by Michael Ende – from the (German) author of *The Never-Ending Story*

PLAYS

Make-Believe by A.A. Milne (Samuel French)

Plays for Children 1 and *Plays for Children 2* (Faber)

POETRY

The New Faber Book of Children's Verse ed. Matthew Sweeney

This anthology has many poems about language and thought, for example: 'A Boy's Head' (Czech) poem by Miroslav Holub; also some in American English (by Shel Silverstein) and some in 'very English' English with a country flavour and fantastic dancing rhythm (Walter de la Mare). There are delicious nonsense poems by Lewis Carroll (in real life Charles Lutwidge Dodgson), author of *Alice in Wonderland*. Irish author Spike Milligan reveals how he liked word-play and humour.

7. A period in history (non-fiction)

An in-depth look at any period that has caught a child's imagination. This can lead to any number of projects, e.g. knights in armour, World War II, history of a country of origin.

8. Historical fiction

Example: unusual slants on World War II (Ages 10–12)

Waiting for Anya by Michael Morpurgo, describes how refugee Jews were smuggled over the Pyrenees into neutral Spain.

I Am David by Ann Holm describes a boy's escape from a German Prison Camp and his journey home.

A similar story from the Far East is *The House of Sixty Fathers* by Meindert de Jong. *The Ice Road* by Jaap ter Haar (Barnowl Books) is about the siege of Leningrad and suitable for age 11 and over.

Here are two more with some matching Teaching Text:

How's Business by Alison Prince: about a UK child evacuee

The British kept their sense of humour. Keeping up the jokes is one way to survive.

Remember that in those days people did not travel as they do now. For centuries most country folk had stayed within a few miles of their own homes, and city folk never saw the country. The War changed all that.

Men in the Forces mixed; richer with poorer, older with younger. Men and women from different parts met and married. Women (including married women, who before the War would have been full-time housewives) had to take on jobs that the men used to do, and when the War was over many wanted to carry on working. Children were evacuated or orphaned; many went short of schooling. There were shortages of food, clothes and books, and furniture. Families were divided by distance and broken up by death.

Society was shuffled like a pack of cards and many were found missing.

Escape from Shangri-La by Michael Morpurgo

Have you ever looked the wrong way down a telescope? Things look very small and far away. For many in this book the War looks just like that, but for one of the characters it still 'looms large' because he hates being in an old folks home and lives for his memories of the D-Day landings. The ending is a surprise.

It is worth considering what is the true meaning of 'Shangri-La'and why it was chosen, also what attitudes to old age prevail. Relationships are significant here.

Grandparents and grandchildren often understand each other well.

The very old and the very young make their own rules.

- -

9. Literature against one or more cultural background
Younger Children
PICTURE BOOKS

Not So Fast Songololo by Niki Daly

Mamo on the Mountain by Jane Kurtz & E.B. Lewis

Hue Boy by Rita Phillips Mitchell, ill. Caroline Binch

The Day of Ahmed's Secret by Florence Parry Heide & Judith Heide Gilliland

Almaz and the Lion by Jane Kurtz and Floyd Cooper

The Elephant's Pillow by Diana Reynold's Roome, ill. Jude Daly

FICTION STORIES

Grandpa Chatterji and *Grandpa's Indian Summer* by Jamila Gavin

Seasons of Splendour by Madhur Jaffrey

PLAY

The Tale of the Red Dragon by Alfred Bradley (Samuel French) This is a Chinese style of play with the stage directions replaced by a person (the Property Man), making it fairly easy to read.

NON-FICTION & POETRY

Whatever is available

Older children (9+)

POETRY

The New Faber Book of Children's Verse ed. Matthew Sweeney

Look for instance at: 'Paper Boats' by Rabindranath Tagore and 'Sea-shell' by William Soutar.

STORY FOR 11+

Princess Jazz and the Angels by Rachel Anderson (Mammoth) India/UK

STORIES FOR 12+

The Other Side of Truth by Beverley Naidoo (Puffin) African /UK

Chandra by Frances Mary Hendry (Oxford) Hindu

Non-fiction could include 'Modern working world'

You could start with the West using the 'Business in Action' series by Cherrytree – Kellogg's; Coca-Cola; McDonald's – and contrast with titles about Third World countries.

. . . .

10. Books *by author*

(including classics and modern classics)

Choose by which author your child is keen on, being careful to see that some titles are not too teenage or adult in emotional content (see Chapter 4). Also choose by which author you would like to introduce, if possible leading into that through the child's current 'topic interests'.

FURTHER RESOURCE 7 Love of Language Course: Part 1 (Age 9+)

You are offered here Part 1 of a two-part course in the history and use of English. Part 1 is a 10-week course. It can be presented to a child as it is; or it can be used page by page in conjunction with any other course, whether fiction or non-fiction.

WORD POWER Unit 1

Name _ _ _ _ _ _ _ _ _ _ _ _ _ _ _ _

In each unit we tell you something we think you ought to know, and give you a chance to practise it.

You need a good dictionary and a thesaurus to help you.

Your dictionary tells you meanings.

It should tell you DERIVATIVES and ORIGINS as well. What are those?

The first is 'the words which come from that word'.

The second is 'where the word came from'.

Your thesaurus gives you a list of words that mean the same, or nearly the same, as the one you started with. You can then choose which is the best for the meaning you want.

FOR YOU TO TRY

In your dictionary find B, find bo..., find

- book
- run your eye down the paragraph following

Is there perhaps a lot more to the word 'BOOK' than you realized?

It is there as a *noun* (an object, a name) but also as a *verb* (an action). You should find more than one definition of each.

You will need access to a dictionary like *Webster's* or the *Oxford Concise* that will give you 'derivatives', in this case the words that have sprung from the word 'book'. You should also be told where the word 'book' came from, in other words its 'origin'.

Good adult dictionaries usually give derivatives and origins in some form but the arrangement may be different on the page.

To understand abbreviations like OFr. or Gmc. see the beginning of your dictionary.

Next turn to your thesaurus

Look up 'book' again! What you are given is not the meaning but a whole list of words associated with 'book'. It gives you 'types of book', and it may lead you straight back to the dictionary to find the meaning of some of the words, like 'compendium' for instance.

Before you leave the thesaurus try looking up another noun, 'hat'.

WORD POWER Unit 2: Words from All the World

Name _ _ _ _ _ _ _ _ _ _ _ _ _ _ _ _ _ _

Have you got your dictionary and a thesaurus by you?

Reminder

Your dictionary tells you meanings.

It should tell you DERIVATIVES and ORIGINS as well.

FOR YOU TO TRY

In your dictionary find the following words and write down which country and language each came from. (For the time being do not concern yourself with how the word arrived in the English language. That comes later.)

beef _

boomerang _

elephant _

fairy _

garage _

mill _

pizza _

radio _

robot _

sari (or saree) _

shop _

sputnik _

tractor _

WORD POWER Unit 3: The Roots of English: Part 1

Name _ _ _ _ _ _ _ _ _ _ _ _ _ _ _ _

Please have both your books to hand.

Last time you looked in your dictionary and got a glimpse of where some words came from.

Did you notice these facts?

1. Some words were very old _

2. Some were words from other languages, adopted by English _ _ _ _ _ _ _
   _

3. Some came into use not very long ago, when something new was invented and needed a name _

4. Quite a number of the words came originally from Latin

   • some through Old English

   • some through Middle English

   • some through Old French or Middle French

   • some by inventing a name based on more modern French (based originally on Latin)

   • some by inventing a new name straight from a known Latin word.

Those Romans certainly had an influence, didn't they?

Next turn to your thesaurus and try looking up a really ancient (OE) adjective: sad.

Its oldest meaning was 'heavy'.

People used to say, 'It went sad' if they took a cake out of the oven before it was quite done and it sank in the middle!

'sad' can mean 'heavy-hearted', can't it?

'sad' in today's world can mean 'unpopular' or 'despised'.

FOR YOU TO TRY

Take some of the words listed in your thesaurus alongside 'sad' and look them up in your dictionary.

Did you find out the source of any?

WORD POWER Unit 4: The Roots of English: Part 2

Name _ _ _ _ _ _ _ _ _ _ _ _ _ _ _ _ _

More information

English was first the language of England. It was brought to America from there.

What you call England got its name from the Angles who invaded what was first called Britain.

In ancient Britain the language was Celtic. Celtic languages of today include

- Breton (from Brittany in France)
- Welsh spoken in Wales (and also in Patagonia, South America!)
- Just a few words of Cornish (in Cornwall, England)
- The Gaelic languages spoken in Ireland and Scotland.

Who else invaded Britain?

1. The Romans
2. The Angles and Saxons
3. The Danes
4. The Vikings
5. The Normans (William the Conqueror, 1066)

That's enough! Let's stop there and look at a few words.

We got a few words from Latin even in those early days. Apart from 'mill' which you know of already, we got 'cheese' and 'street' and 'tile'. Doesn't that tell you about Romans being civilized?

Anglo-Saxon used to be the name of everything 'English'

You remember it's where the word 'English' came from! That first English language used to be called Anglo-Saxon but is now known as Old English (OE).

From it we have many ordinary everyday words like 'mother' and 'father' and 'child'; 'house' and 'land'; 'heart' and 'head'; 'weeping' and 'laughing', too.

There are place names like Kingston, which came from OE 'cyninges tun' meaning 'king's village'.

The Danes and the Vikings spoke Germanic languages not too different from that of the Angles and Saxons but they did give us some new words, too.

Listen to this. The OE word for a tunic gave us the modern 'shirt', while the Viking version became a 'skirt'!

WORD POWER Unit 5: The Roots of English: Part 3

Name _ _ _ _ _ _ _ _ _ _ _ _ _ _ _ _ _ _

FOR YOU TO TRY

Choose ONE or MORE of these (OE origin) words and turn to your thesaurus to find out what other words in modern English have the same or a similar meaning.

NOUNS head, heart, child

VERBS weep, laugh, sit, stand, speak

ADJECTIVES bright, idle, great, small

ADVERBS down, up, lightly, well

_ _

_ _

_ _

_ _

Maybe look up one or two of the other words in your dictionary?

The Normans

It's a strange thing about the Normans. They were originally 'Northmen' who had come south and settled in what we now call France. But they had largely taken on the language of their adopted country! So when they conquered England they brought with them the kind of French they spoke.

For a while the existing Old English remained separate from the language of the conquerors. The poor man tended the 'swine' and the 'sheep' while the rich man ate the 'pork' and the 'mutton'!

It took over a century for the two languages to gradually come together as one. This version of English is now known as Middle English. It is important to know that it varied a great deal from one part of the country to another. How do we know? Well we have writings from that time, just as we do from Anglo-Saxon times.

From what the Normans brought we have derived hundreds of modern words:

- not only 'duke', 'baron', 'warden', and 'venison' (from the conquerors' lifestyle)

- but also words like 'flowers', 'beauty', 'notice', and 'clear'.

Note: English took on thousands more French words in later times.

WORD POWER Unit 6: Words from the Languages of Other Countries

Name _ _ _ _ _ _ _ _ _ _ _ _ _ _ _ _ _ _ _

You know quite a bit about this already. You know about the words invaders brought centuries ago, and in Unit 1 you looked up some 'foreign' words from recent times.

Words direct from French

English has gone on taking in words from French at various times in history. Some centuries after the Normans gave us 'warden' and 'ward', we took on 'guardian' and 'guard' which were really the same words in a slightly altered form. The meaning is similar but not quite the same, is it?

All through the centuries French words have crept in, because of wars, because of royal marriages, because of fashion in clothes and food.

Words direct from Latin

English has gone on taking in words from Latin, first through the influence of the Church in Rome, then through the rediscovery of the literature and art of the ancient world (known as the Renaissance – a French word meaning 're-birth').

Words direct from Greek

English has taken many words from the Greek of the Bible and from ancient Greek (from the time of the Renaissance in particular).

English has made up words using bits of Latin and Greek.

FOR YOU TO TRY

In your dictionary find out where these came from:

fruit	_ _ _ _ _ _ _ _ _ _ _ _	chaos	_ _ _ _ _ _ _ _ _ _ _ _
serviette	_ _ _ _ _ _ _ _ _ _ _ _	curriculum	_ _ _ _ _ _ _ _ _ _ _ _
cigarette	_ _ _ _ _ _ _ _ _ _ _ _	telephone	_ _ _ _ _ _ _ _ _ _ _ _
chocolate	_ _ _ _ _ _ _ _ _ _ _ _	metamorphosis	_ _ _ _ _ _ _ _ _ _ _ _

Thesaurus: Which of these means anything like the Greek word 'chaos'?

'muddle' 'mess' 'confusion' 'disorder' ' disarray' 'tip'

True story:

Teenager   *(answering the phone)*: 'I'm sorry?'

Caller: I said, 'Is that the tip?'

Teenager: 'The only tip here is my room. You can have that if you like!'

WORD POWER Unit 7: Choosing the Word You Really Want

Name _ _ _ _ _ _ _ _ _ _ _ _ _ _ _ _

FOR YOU TO TRY

Your thesaurus should help you find the best word to use.

Look up the word 'care' and see what other words your thesaurus gives you alongside that word.

Here are some sentences that require you to choose the best word from your list. 'Care' might be all right in all the spaces. If it sounds right put it in. Otherwise look for an alternative word.

1. He took _ _ _ _ _ _ _ _ _ _ _ _ _ to see that his sister had enough food even if he had to do without.

2. I do not _ _ _ _ _ _ _ _ _ _ _ _ which I have.

3. The cares and _ _ _ _ _ _ _ _ _ _ _ _ of a lifetime had left their mark on those faces.

4. 'Caroline is an orphan,' he explained, 'and is under the _ _ _ _ _ _ _ _ _ _ _ _ of her uncle.'

Something you might like to know:

People, whatever their language, can understand more words than they ever think of using.

Make sure you understand the words you hear other people use, and the words you read. Here are some that have been used in this course so far:

derivative *n*.

originally *adv*.

ancient *adj*

venison *n*.

WORD POWER Unit 8: Using New Words in Speaking and Writing

Name _ _ _ _ _ _ _ _ _ _ _ _ _ _ _ _ _

FOR YOU TO TRY

Turn to your thesaurus. Can you find slightly better or alternative words for any of those in bold in the sentences below?

1. The surgeon decided the patient needed a **very big** operation

   _

2. The magistrate gave his **view** that the woman was guilty

   _

3. The boys' bedrooms were in a terrible **disorder**

   _

4. The cat gave signs that it wanted to **exit**

   _

5. The man's voice was so faint it was practically **impossible to hear**

   _

You probably did this with words that you didn't just 'know' (in the sense of 'recognize'), but words you knew how to use.

In some cases you will have chosen a simpler word (that has probably been a long time in the language), and in others something much grander (a relative newcomer).

Maybe you replaced one word with two, or the other way round?

Choosing the right (the best, the most appropriate, the most apt) word is something which comes with practice.

Using words

People use the words they have stored away in their memories as 'active vocabulary'.

This vocabulary or 'word store' will be less than the store of words they can understand (or comprehend[1]).

You can try to make your active vocabulary bigger! Please do.

Using words is a very important business. Sometimes choosing just the right word to say what you mean, or write what you want to, can make a lot of difference to the way others hear you and understand.

Have you ever 'made a speech'?

---

1   Notice the link with 'comprehension', the word used for the work you do in school when you read a passage and answer questions to show that you have understood.

WORD POWER Unit 9: Quoting

Name _ _ _ _ _ _ _ _ _ _ _ _ _ _ _ _ _ _

When you read a non-fiction book or encyclopedia to get information about a topic you can react in several ways

1. You can keep the information in your head and think about it.

2. You can speak about it or discuss it.

3. You can make notes in writing,

   - either recording the information in your own words

   - or copying the words in front of you.

This last one counts as 'quoting', because you are using somebody else's words.

If you are using somebody else's words then you are obliged to acknowledge that fact, and the right and proper way to do it is to put 'quotation marks' at the beginning and end of the passage you are borrowing or quoting.

This is very important. You could be actually breaking the law if you don't!

Then to finish off your acknowledgement that these words were not your own, you give the title and author of the book you quoted from. Either you put it in brackets straight after the quote or you put it in a footnote.

Generally it is best to absorb the information and write about it in your own words

We call this using 'indirect' or 'reported' speech.

An example follows so that you can see how it starts with the writer Hugh Graham reporting what a famous author said, but using his own words. Then he quotes the next words of the author as she said them.

Note that the person writing your WORD POWER course had to get permission for quoting both paragraphs!

Here are the two paragraphs [from an article published in a writers' magazine]

The first part is written by Hugh Graham, the person writing the article. He recounts in reported speech what the famous author said in a talk at the writers' conference…

> P.D. James has written nineteen thrillers and says all authors should read and read because it will improve their writing. She thinks we are lucky to write in English because so many people know it and will read our work.

Then Hugh Graham continues the article, this time quoting P.D. James' own words:

> 'Extend your vocabulary. English can convey wonderful shades of meaning and the precise choice of a word ensures that our readers understand precisely what we are trying to say. When we are reading, the dictionary and thesaurus should be constant companions. Should we have any doubt about the precise meaning of a word it is our duty to check it out and then to consider alternatives…'

> *Writers' Forum*, October/November 2001, Hugh Graham quoting the words of P.D. James in his report on the Winchester Writers' Conference.

NOTE

For the WORD POWER author to be allowed to quote both of these paragraphs from Hugh Graham's article, she had to get permission from the magazine called *Writers' Forum*, and the magazine had previously got permission from P.D. James for her exact words to be quoted.

This is copyright law. The copyright sign, by the way, is © and is followed by the copyright owner's name.

Incidentally, P.D. James was likewise reported to have said that punctuation is equally important.

That's another subject, but you might like to consider and discuss it.

WORD POWER Unit 10: Summary

This final unit allows you to show in your own words what you have gained from Part 1 of your Love of Language Course.

Name _ _ _ _ _ _ _ _ _ _ _ _ _ _ _ _

A dictionary gives you _

_ _

_ _

_ _

A thesaurus is helpful in _

_ _

_ _

_ _

_ _

Tick any words which were new to you and add a few more of your own

precise   quoting   acknowledge   warden   guardianship   swine
mutton   disarray   chaos   curriculum   metamorphosis   thesaurus

_____

_____

_____

_____

What was the most interesting part of your WORD POWER course?

_____

_____

_____

_____

FURTHER RESOURCE 8 Love of Language Course: Part 2 (Age 10+)

This is also a 10-week course, and was originally written for one year later than Part 1 but could follow on if the student is thought to be sufficiently mature.

LOOK AT LANGUAGE Unit 1: Juggling with Words – 'Communication'

In Part 1 we talked about using your dictionary and thesaurus, and followed up with a page each week on 'where English words came from' (ORIGINS), with hints on how to pick exactly the word you wish to use.

We could sum up in these words:

Language is interesting. It has deep roots. It is alive, and it changes with time.

In Part 2 we are ready to share with you more information about English.

Language is the way we say what we want to say. We use it to communicate with others.

We have to ask or tell, in speech or in writing, whatever we need to convey; we have to rely on the understanding of the person who is listening to or reading our words. When politicians appear in front of the cameras to report on the latest developments, they have to choose what they say with immense care, for several reasons:

- because of the huge numbers of people who will hear them, and whose thoughts and attitudes will depend on what their leaders have told them

- so that they are clear and unequivocal, and their words cannot be twisted in the press or on radio and television

- because in times of crisis the words of leaders are written down and may be quoted in the future, becoming part of history, e.g. Winston Churchill's words on UK radio during the Second World War, 'We will fight them on the beaches...'

But if you, or anybody else, either gives a speech, or writes a message or article, that is only one side of the communication process. The other side is the hearing and understanding (comprehension) of those who receive these words.

It pays to have a good vocabulary! Did you know the word 'unequivocal'? If not, did you look in your dictionary?

Here are some more words with a negative tone, in this case telling us that communication has broken down, either at the speaking/writing end or at the listening/reading end. They all begin with what we call a PREFIX. A prefix is attached to the beginning of a word and changes its meaning.

inaudible **in**comprehensible **in**ept **un**heard **dis**regarded **dis**missed

Note that the prefixes, and rest of the words, have various origins.

LOOK AT LANGUAGE Unit 2: Juggling with Words – 'Meanings 1'

Prefixes

Try to match the prefixes in List 1 with the words in List 2.

Hint: look up the meaning of the prefixes first, and do not neglect their origins. (The length of time a word has been part of our language affects the ease with which we use and understand that word. Example: 'an affair of the heart' would not be the same if we said 'a cardiac affair', would it? 'Cardiac' makes us think of hospitals, not love!)

1. 'pre' 'de' 'dis' and 'sub'

2. _____ frost   _____ marine

   _____ agree   _____ way

   _____ honest   _____ paid

   _____ construct

Think a little about the context in which you would use these words.

Notice that some of the words you built are nouns and some are verbs.

Meanings and deeper meanings

Look at these verbs: 'build' and 'construct'. Decide for yourself: Is their meaning exactly the same? Look at their origins. Which is older? Which of those two words would you be more likely to use metaphorically? If you are not sure, pick the one you would use to complete this sentence:

The idea of bringing people in the community together is to break down barriers and _____ relationships.

See if you can discover SHADES OF MEANING in these pairs of SYNONYMS.

(A SYNONYM is 'the same' or 'very nearly the same' in meaning).

> 'same' and 'identical'
>
> 'warm' and 'tepid'
>
> 'beach' and 'shore'
>
> 'synthetic' and 'artificial'

Be aware that one word can have more than one meaning.

Not so very long ago, everyone was discussing the attack on the World Trade Center in New York and the 'War on Terrorism'. They were using the word 'intelligence' in a sense that is different from 'whether a person is 'brainy' or not'!

Try to think of circumstances where you would use 'intelligence' to mean 'brain power', and others where you want the word to refer to secret information coming in.

LOOK AT LANGUAGE Unit 3: Juggling with Words – 'Word-building'

More prefixes (these are all negative)

un-, in- or im-, non-

Add each prefix to a suitable word below:

_____do   _____decisive   _____mature   _____smoker

Perhaps do some more research in this area using the dictionary. List any especially interesting words you find.

_____

_____

Now let's look at suffixes

These are 'building blocks' that go on the end of a word. First try a few, and then we can look more closely at what is happening here:

_____dom   _____ness   _____hood   _____ment

'Adding bits on the end' brings us into the area where words are closely related, the area that is to a certain extent covered by the DERIVATIVES section in your dictionary. When you add a suffix you may be creating a new noun, or changing an adjective into a noun.

How can you change an adjective into an adverb? _____

_____

Examples?

_ _

_ _

_ _

Sometimes a new word is created with a prefix and other building blocks that are equally old:

Example: 'oneupmanship'.

Sometimes prefixes and suffixes come from a source that is not the same as

the word to which they are attached. Example?

_ _

_ _

_ _

_ _

LOOK AT LANGUAGE Unit 4: Juggling with Words – 'Spelling 1'

OK. So spelling may not be a problem for you. There are still some interesting things to learn however, and (surprise, surprise!) a lot of it is to do with where the word came from.

A long time ago you will have been shown that a noun that ends in 'y' in the singular, will very likely change to 'ies' in the plural…

Rules about when to make this change and when not

Find out all you can from this passage:

> 'If the baby cries, do something to stop it crying. Nobody likes it when babies cry. It's a strange thing, but once you bring a smile to a baby's face it will look as though it never cried in its life.'

Note how not only the noun but also the verb changes from 'y' to 'ies' or 'ied'. And, as you probably know by now, using an apostrophe is not the way to multiply a baby! The apostrophe + s in the phrase 'a baby's face' means the face belongs to a baby.

Now try underscoring all the words which illustrate what we have just been telling you!

Question: So when does a 'y' stand firm and remain itself even when an 's' is added on?

Answer: when it has a vowel in front of it.

Examples: toys, and donkeys

The guys had lost their keys.

They had not seen any monkeys of that kind for several days.

A couple of cases where the ORIGIN is the clue to the spelling

Ph words come from Greek: photograph, telephone, phonic.

Kn words are Germanic: knife, knight, knee.

And this one was William's fault!

In OE, words we now spell with 'gh' before the 't' had just an 'h' and that was pronounced the way modern German pronounces 'ch' in its word 'Licht' meaning 'light'.

William Caxton (1421–1491) brought printing to England from Holland where they used not just 'h' for this sound but 'gh'. So 'gh' came to England with Caxton's printing press, and is still there, even though we don't say it any more!

Examples: bright light; weight and height; he thought he ought.

LOOK AT LANGUAGE Unit 5: Juggling with Words – 'Spelling 2'

Two Rules – one which gets broken

1. The letter C consistently sounds like K
   - when followed by O or A or U
   - when followed by R or L

Examples: constant, caterwaul, cubicle, crazy, cluttered

The letter C mostly sounds like S (sometimes like 'sh')
   - when followed by E or I

Examples: city, centre, science, noticeable, conscientious

2. The letter G ought to follow the same rule as C.

Often it does:
   - got, gate, gust, great, glad, vague
   - gentle, giant

But here are some common 'misfits':

> 'girls get the giggles'

Some people find it hard to spell 'gorgeous' or 'Geoffrey' but at least the letter G in these words obeys the rule!

The spelling affects the meaning and vice versa

Examples:

> eyesight and building site;

> stomach pain and window pane.

Take a careful look at this:

> 'They're never there in time for their supper.'

Something more subtle

Did the glass slipper fit Cinderella? Yes, it fitted perfectly.

But 'benefited' has only one 't' because the stress is on another syllable.

Hapy Speling ! (?)

LOOK AT LANGUAGE Unit 6: Juggling with Words – 'Meanings 2'

We began with this statement:

> Language is interesting. It has deep roots. It is alive, and changes with time.

Now let us add a further statement that will make this week's focus meaningful:

> Language is the way we say what we want to say. We use it to COMMUNICATE with others.

We need to speak (or write) clearly in a language that the other person can understand. To do that, we need to choose our words. And to do that we need a good stock of words from which to choose, words that we understand.

Lots of words have more than one meaning, even simple words like: cut; play; toy. Explore these as nouns or verbs, using your dictionary.

Another example: 'mind'

1. My big sister has to mind the baby while Mum's at work.
2. 'Mind if I borrow your bike?'
3. 'What exactly did you have in mind?'

The true search for meaning begins with the ORIGIN of the word.

Try finding out where these came from:

shield _____

honour _____

home _____

field _____

noble _____

tea _____

persistence _____

investigation _____

Because of all the languages English has taken words from we often have a choice of words from different roots. Sometimes either will do. Sometimes choosing the one that really fits will help you to convey your meaning more clearly.

Think hard about these pairs of words:

> house/home
>
> old/ancient
>
> clear/lucid
>
> sad/miserable
>
> brains/intelligence

Sometimes either would do. Other times the particular flavour of one of those words makes it the better one to use.

LOOK AT LANGUAGE Unit 7: Juggling with Words – 'The Right Word 1'

Well, the right word for what?

Think for a minute of all the ways we communicate:

- holding a conversation with one or more people in the same space
- telephoning
- making a speech to a group gathered in front of you
- speaking on radio or television
- writing a letter (snail-mail)
- e-mailing
- text messaging
- writing in a newspaper or magazine
- writing a book (non-fiction)
- writing a short story or novel
- writing a play
- writing a poem
- writing for yourself (shopping list, homework notes, diary).

The first division is between SPEAKING and WRITING.

SPEAKING does not give you second chances. You have to say, here and now, exactly what you want to get across. 'Don't say anything you'll regret' is a good motto.

The words you use will come from that 'stock' which is known as your 'ACTIVE vocabulary', the words you know and understand well enough to use, as opposed to the words you can comprehend when you hear or read them but have never used (your PASSIVE vocabulary).

WRITING slows you down. You have time to think a little. Especially if you are working on the computer you get a chance to change things when you have an 'afterthought'.

Before you start writing you will probably have time to make a plan, even if it is only in your head.

LOOK AT LANGUAGE Unit 8: Juggling with Words – 'The Right Word 2'

Train yourself to speak and write clearly, by

1. thinking (and making notes) clearly, logically and systematically

2. knowing and fully understanding a large number of words

3. finding out which word fits best.

Thinking logically

Some people learn best by hearing, and some by seeing. Most like something of both.

First work out if you are predominantly a 'word thinker' or a 'picture thinker'.

This will help you find out how to order your thoughts (whether in words or in a picture/diagram/chart).

You need to make a conscious effort to build your vocabulary, both the 'passive' (word recognition) kind and the 'active' kind. You also need to work at moving words from the passive side of memory to the active.

Use your dictionary. Use your thesaurus. Many famous speakers and established writers still do.

Word practice

Find two words in the list which could mean the same [SYNONYMs] and two more which could mean the opposite [ANTONYMs] of each word in bold below.

precisely: exactly, truly, responsibly, carelessly, vaguely, hopelessly

happy: sunny, joyful, breezy, miserable, vicious, downhearted

Finally you are invited to think about whether the words in each pair below always mean the same, or if they can have slightly different meanings, or be used on different occasions:

> multiply/increase
>
> cover/protect

hide/conceal

interfere/step in

barge in/intrude

help/assist

(Discuss with a friend or adult mentor if you need to.)

Can you make up more pairs of this kind?

LOOK AT LANGUAGE Unit 9: Juggling with Words – 'Say What You Mean 1'

'Think before you speak' is surely related to 'Look before you leap'!

When you speak, either you have to have thought out beforehand what you are going to say, or you have to think and speak almost simultaneously.

When you write, you generally slow down and have time to think before you put pen to paper or type the next line.

Clear thinking is obviously important.

If you think in words then you need words even for your own thoughts!

Great thinkers, speakers and writers have left us famous words. Take a look at any good book of quotations.

We quote famous words because they have behind them the authority of the people who first said them. Shakespeare is a prime example. Did you know that many things first written by him are now part of our everyday speech?

Examples: vanished into thin air; the game is up; fair play; bloody-minded.

STYLE comes in to your speaking and writing, too. We shall be saying more about that later.

But first we want to show you the importance of that little 'box of tools' we call punctuation. What is in it?

>   the comma
>
>   the period (full stop)
>
>   the capital letter
>
>   the colon and semi-colon
>
>   the question mark
>
>   the exclamation mark
>
>   brackets (round or square) and
>
>   inverted commas (single or double)

Nowadays schools give plenty of practice in the use of these, we know. We just want to focus on the humble comma for a moment and illustrate how its use or misuse changes meaning.

1. The cow jumped over the moon, while the little dog laughed and the dish ran away.

2. The cow jumped, while over the moon the little dog laughed, and the dish ran away.

3. The cow jumped, while over the moon the little dog laughed and the dish ran away.

Who was over the moon in each case?

Consider where you would insert a comma in this advertisement so that the legs belonged to the piano rather than to the lady.

WANTED. A piano for a lady with carved legs.

Alternatively you could change the WORD ORDER. Word order is another thing that affects the meaning. Think about that. There is an example in the next unit.

LOOK AT LANGUAGE Unit 10: Juggling with Words – 'Say What You Mean 2' Arrangements and Styles

You probably learned long ago what we call parts of speech. On this course you've been left to pick up for yourselves whether the word you were looking at was a noun, a verb, an adjective or an adverb.

The cat sat on the mat. Remember? You could change that statement bit by bit until you finished up with 'All afternoon the lazy Persian posed on the tiger-skin hearthrug' (or something of the kind).

But a few tiny words remain to be mentioned. 'The' is the 'definite article'; 'a' or 'an' the indefinite article.

Prepositions you learned when you were very young but it is unlikely you knew their official name: on, at, with, in, by, over, under …

Conjunctions: the clue is in the word itself. They are 'links'. You start with 'and' and 'but' when you are very young.

Examples: Jack and Jill.

She came downstairs and helped herself to breakfast.

He promised much but did little.

Bear in mind that these are the very simplest of the conjunctions.

Try thinking hard about other words which join sentences together.

Example: She worked on, while he sat reading the paper.

Use all these tools carefully. Your dictionary will inform you.

Here's the promised bit about WORD ORDER (discovered in an extract from a hospital letter):

'Please make sure you arrange what time to collect the patient before leaving the hospital with a nurse.' (Free nurse with every visit?!)

Can you cleverly re-shuffle the phrases so that the true meaning is clear?

Help! Time is running out! Just a quick word about STYLE.

We're not talking here about the particular style of each author, which you recognize as his or her 'voice'.

Instead we want to draw your attention to 'jargon' and 'slang', and the patterns of speech which have to come to us from the past or are being invented in our own time.

Cockney rhyming slang: Use your loaf! ('Loaf of bread' = 'head')

Texting: C U later!

Appendix 1

The Legacy of Charlotte Mason 1842–1923

The school's aim is to carry on the philosophy of Charlotte Mason by making learning enjoyable and creating an environment where children will be safe, stimulated and challenged. A place where fun and enjoyment go hand in hand with learning and discovery.

(From the website of St. Agnes PNEU Nursery School, Headingley: quoted with permission.)

Charlotte Mason has been mentioned more than once in the pages of my book. While I do not claim that Open Way principles are based directly on what she has to say in her many books, which are still available today, it is true that the freedom she advocated in her approach to living and learning was something I recognized as valuable and right.

She has been described as 'an extraordinary educator whose thinking looked to the significance of atmosphere, habit and living ideas' (see www.infed.org.uk/thinkers/et-mason.htm). Time spent reading about this far-sighted woman will be time well spent.

Who was Charlotte Mason?

She was born in Wales at a time when new ideas about education and the rights of women and girls were beginning to creep in on the traditional, formal scene of classical schooling for boys. She was a keen reader and was trained in the methods of Johann Pestalozzi. Her parents died and left her an independent woman at only 16. She eventually founded her own teacher training college, a high school for girls and the national organization known as PNEU (Parents' National Education Union) and elementary schools.

What was her influence?
IN MAINSTREAM, STATE/PUBLIC EDUCATION

Few people realize how much of Charlotte Mason's thinking crept into elementary-age education as a whole during the 20th century, for example the importance of

- studying nature (and engaging in other outdoor activities)
- learning languages
- music, drama and speech training
- art and craft.

IN OTHER AREAS OF EDUCATION

You can find Charlotte Mason's principles apparent:

- in various PNEU and independent schools (for ages anywhere from 3 to 18)
- at college level – she founded St. Martin's College in Ambleside UK which became a state-run College of Education still demonstrating her principles, and today is the site of the University of Cumbria; one trainee of the original college founded a school still here today
- in USA home-schooling and home education worldwide.

For more information on Charlotte Mason try the following websites:

www.infed.org.uk/thinkers/et-mason.htm

www.simplycharlottemason.com

www.westfield.newcastle.sch.uk/our_history.asp

www.marcusbicknell.co.uk/obh/obh3.htm

www.amblesideonline.org

Appendix 2

Writing for Use on a Larger Scale

Writing for distance-learning

Perhaps when you have successfully run a course with a known child or group you might feel like becoming author and mentor for other children? Open Way began as such a 'distance-learning course' – I wrote for unknown children and sold courses to families, thereafter acting as mentor. This meant operating largely on a 'one size fits all' basis, with a kind of 'alterations service' to meet the needs of a particular child. It will certainly be easier for you to start small and afterwards extend if you wish.

Here are some things to bear in mind when creating a distance-learning course:

- You will be finding books for children you have never met, and therefore need to suit all tastes, giving titles that families will be likely to find (particularly in libraries, as otherwise the cost would be too high for most).

- Some families may want to buy a book list only, or will ask to buy your materials to run themselves, without yourself as mentor. In this situation you will miss out on getting to know the child and gauging his or her tastes and needs.

- If you become a mentor, Teaching Text will be the only way you have of communicating with the child. (See samples in Chapter 3 and Further Resource 5.)

- To give good value as mentor you will also need to write a fairly lengthy 'Mentor's Reply' [see p.54] engaging the child and allowing the parent to see how you are responding to their child's views.

- I recommend giving parents a Report (along the lines of Reading, Response and Forecast as designed for schools) half-way through a batch of 18 units, and again at the end.

- You could devise a Certificate for the pupil at the end of each course level.

Engaging others to write/mentor alongside yourself

It is plausible to engage other writers to produce such modules on the same lines as your own, choosing their own area of enthusiasm. This has led, in the past, to a wide variety of themes: China; English Grammar; Rivers; Poetry; Story-writing; and Historical Fiction. You can pay such other writer an initial fee for use of copyright over a given period, with option to renew by mutual agreement after let's say three years. You will not then be 'an employer', and eventually the copyright will revert to the writer. Writers who join you must be in tune with gifted children and understand Open Way principles; they can act as mentors but should be paid 'tuition fees' rather than a wage.

Writing for sale to other educators

This is another way of extending. You can offer a course you would use yourself.

- If dealing with schools, most of the books you give on your list at the time of sale should be in print and only a few marked 'Library only'. You will need to give ISBN and price.
- If you are to be provider for say a chain of schools or a group of home-schooling families then your course will be sold on a 'one-off' basis and your book lists will be all right for that time and place and last for ever.
- If you wish to sell the course over time then, for your own records at least, keep track of your titles by publisher. You can then check periodically whether each book you recommended last year is still in print now. And you can more easily find out what new titles you might use to 'refurbish' a topic.

Operating on a large scale

Beyond the small-scale course that my book is intended to help you create, the only real way to operate successfully is to be asked and authorized to write on such a large scale that you will be able to:

- make yourself widely known
- guarantee enough sales to persuade publishers to hold in print the books you wish to use.

I would say that to reach this point you need to gain widespread official recognition and support.

Appendix 3

Further Reading for Adults

Books on reading and education

Barrs, M. and Cork, V. (2001) *The Reader in the Writer: The Links Between the Study of Literature and Writing Development at Key Stage 2*. London: Centre for Language in Primary Education.

Dean, G. (1998) *Challenging the More Able Language User*. London: NACE/David Fulton Publishers.

Distin, K. (ed.) (2006) *Gifted Children: A Guide for Parents and Professionals*. London: Jessica Kingsley Publishers.

Eyre, D. and McClure, L. (eds) (2001) *Curriculum Provision for the Gifted and Talented in the Primary School: English, Maths, Science and ICT*. London: NACE/David Fulton Publishers.

Gatto, J.T. (2001) *A Different Kind of Teacher: Solving the Crisis of American Schooling*. Albany, CA: Berkeley Hills Books.

Leyden, S. (2002) *Supporting the Child of Exceptional Ability* (3rd edition). London: NACE/David Fulton Publishers.

Reference books

Watson, V. (2001) *The Cambridge Guide to Children's Books in English*. Cambridge: Cambridge University Press.

Carpenter, H. and Mari Pritchard, M. (1999) *The Oxford Companion to Children's Literature*. Oxford: Oxford University Press

Websites

www.anpeip.org (France)

www.dpsk12.org/departments/gt/resources.html (US)

www.giftedchildren.org.nz (New Zealand)

www.mensa.org.za/magic.asp (South Africa)

www.nace.co.uk (UK)

www.nagcbritain.org.uk (UK)

www.nagc.org (US)

www.parentscentre.gov.uk/educationandlearning/whatchildrenlearn/specialcircumstances/giftedtaletedchildren (UK)

www.ygt.dcsf.gov.uk (UK)

Index